What People Are Saying

True Evange...

Bishop John writes out of the deep experience of a varied, dedicated and distinguished ministry with the authority of a life shaped by scholarship and scripture. This is a quietly passionate book, it is important, timely and it flows out of a generous heart.
The Very Revd David Hoyle, Dean of Westminster Abbey

Bishop John and I grew up in the same Anglo-Catholic Church in Brightlingsea in Essex and have been life-long friends. Now both of us, well past retirement age, look out at a radically changed and still changing Anglican Church and neither of us is convinced that it is wise to ignore the DNA that makes the Anglican Church distinctive and holds the potential for resilience in an age in which the Christian narrative is no longer strong in society. Bishop John has written a timely book that addresses a cry from the heart shaped, as all best Anglican theology is, on the anvil of lived experience interpreted in the light of scripture and in the light of tradition.
Professor Leslie Francis

Bishop John's Apologia for a humane evangelicalism should be read by anyone who cherishes the Evangelical and the Anglican tradition, not least those who might be tempted to dub him a "back-slider". In earlier days after an Anglo-Catholic upbringing, he acknowledges coming to a living faith in Jesus but also a somewhat independent ecclesiology. He has since argued for a deeper Anglican ecclesiology which gives space for the experience of Christians as members of the Body of Christ. All members of the Church are in St Paul's words "in Christ" and part of the community or communion of the Church. This experience means that doctrine is not static. Tradition is a living and changing experience. This does not mean that anything goes because the *consensus fidelium* remains subject to Scripture. At the same time Scripture and tradition require a hermeneutic. Bishop John thus pleads for a generous orthodoxy which is expressed in an Anglican tradition of ordered liturgy composed of Word and Sacrament. The mission of the local parish must be to serve the whole community rather than become a gathered congregation of the elect. This will require a new evangelism of the Pilgrim Church by definition, far from static. After setting out this manifesto, Bishop John expounds the detail chapter by chapter and deals with the particular, sometimes contested issues. This courageous theological autobiography is highly relevant to contemporary Church of England Evangelicals and all Anglicans in a divided communion.

The Right Revd Christopher Hill, retired Bishop of Guildford, co-secretary of the Anglican-Roman Catholic International Commission (1974–1981) and one time President of the Council of European Churches

In this personal and theologically sensitive reflection on his ministry and the changes affecting the Church during his time, Bishop John makes an eloquent and persuasive appeal to the Church of England to re-engage with the distinctive contribution of Evangelical Anglicanism to the Church of Christ. This will be encouraging reading to many within that tradition but also to the Anglican Communion's Ecumenical partners.

Judith Lieu, Lady Margaret's Professor of Divinity Emerita, University of Cambridge, Methodist lay preacher and former chair of the Methodist Faith and Order Committee

This short book of wisdom drawn from Bishop John Went's life and ministry as an Anglican Evangelical offers an important

voice into a divided Church. It challenges those who are serious about following Scripture within the Church of England's Evangelical tradition to do so in a way which serves the Church rather than divides it. Bishop John pulls few punches in his observations about recent developments in the Church's mission, which makes this a significant contribution, worth reading across the breadth of the Church but especially by those who share his own Evangelical commitment both in the Church of England but also those of an Evangelical tradition in other denominations.
The Very Revd John Witcombe, Dean of Coventry Cathedral

The Church of England faces new challenges alongside questions on which Christians are deeply divided. This is the context within which we are called to proclaim the gospel afresh. In his timely book Bishop John offers us a great gift. He reminds us that there are within Anglican theology and ecclesiology truths that can enable us as Christians while holding significantly different theological and ecclesiological views to remain in fellowship with one another. He shares a vision of a Church of England that is united at the same time as allowing for an enormous richness of diversity. It is a vision rooted in scripture, Anglican tradition and deep theological reflection; a vision which offers the Church of Jesus Christ a compelling model of a community of rich diversity being united in the love of God, Father, Son and Holy Spirit for the sake of a divided and hurting world.
The Right Revd Dr Michael Volland, former Principal of Ridley Hall, Bishop of Birmingham

True Evangelical

The Changing Face of Anglican Evangelicalism

True Evangelical

The Changing Face of Anglican Evangelicalism

Bishop John Went Reflects on a Lifetime of Discipleship and Ministry

CHRISTIAN ALTERNATIVE
BOOKS

Winchester, UK
Washington, USA

CollectiveInk

First published by Christian Alternative Books, 2025
Christian Alternative Books is an imprint of Collective Ink, Ltd.
Unit 11, Shepperton House, 89
Shepperton Road, London, N1 3DF
office@collectiveinkbooks.com
www.collectiveinkbooks.com
www.christian-alternative.com

For distributor details and how to order please visit the 'Ordering' section on our website.

Text copyright: John Went

ISBN: 978 1 80341 695 3
978 1 80341 788 2 (ebook)
Library of Congress Control Number: 2024931797

All rights reserved. Except for brief quotations in critical articles or reviews, no part of this book may be reproduced in any manner without prior written permission from the publishers.

The rights of John Went as author have been asserted in accordance with the Copyright, Designs and Patents Act 1988.

A CIP catalogue record for this book is available from the British Library.

Design: Lapiz Digital Services

UK: Printed and bound by CPI Group (UK) Ltd, Croydon, CR0 4YY
US: Printed and bound by Thomson-Shore, 7300 West Joy Road, Dexter, MI 48130

We operate a distinctive and ethical publishing philosophy in all areas of our business, from our global network of authors to production and worldwide distribution.

Contents

Chapter 1: The Changing Face of Anglican Evangelicalism   1
   I. Do Church of England Evangelicals Stand in a Purely Reformed Tradition?   4
   II. The Relationship of Scripture and Tradition   7
   III. History of the Term *Anglican*   10
   IV. Characteristics of Anglican Theology   12

Chapter 2: The Central Place of the Bible in Anglicanism and Evangelical Theology   20
   I. The Place of the Bible in the Reformation and Pre-Reformation Trailblazers   20
   II. Various Factors in the Anglican Tradition Influence the Interpretation of the Bible   22
   III. The Evangelical Revival, and the Bible and Preaching Ministry   23

Chapter 3: An Anglican Evangelical Holding Together Word and Sacrament   29
   I. Eucharistic or Non-Eucharistic Interpretation of the Emmaus Road Story and John 6?   30
   II. Keele Congress and Anglican Evangelicals' Placing More Emphasis on the Eucharist at the Centre of Sunday Worship   33
   III. Is There Only One Way of Preaching Biblically?   36
   IV. A Bible-based Approach to Giving   38
   V. Preaching Related to a Building Project over and against Preaching on the Lectionary   39
   VI. Word and Sacrament Together Increasingly Part of My Own Spiritual Life   41

Chapter 4: Christian Belief Shaped through Prayer and Liturgy — 43
I. Cranmer's 1662 Prayer Book and Liturgical Reform in the Twentieth Century — 43
II. Changed Understanding of the Relationship between the Eucharist and the Cross — 46
III. Anglican Worship: Liturgical Rather Than Free — 48
IV. Liturgy Shaping Theology — 48
V. The Place of Scripture in Anglican Liturgy — 50

Chapter 5: Evangelicals and the Challenge of Hermeneutics — 51
I. Biblical Hermeneutics in the Latter Years of the Twentieth Century — 53
II. An Application to the Ordination of Women as Priests and Bishops — 55
III. Reflections on the Nature of Christian Unity — 56
IV. Ecumenical Experience at Tantur in Jerusalem, Enriching My Own Christian Understanding — 58

Chapter 6: Evangelicals and a Commitment to Evangelism — 64
I. Evangelism among Young People — 67
II. Evangelism Explosion: Lessons Learned from an American Presbyterian Church — 69
III. The Gospel as Cross-Shaped — 76
IV. Focus on Evangelism as an Archdeacon and Suffragan Bishop — 81

Chapter 7: Understanding Mission on a Broad Canvas — 84
I. The Lausanne Conferences and Holistic Mission — 84
II. TEAR Fund Founded in 1968 — 87

III. Holistic Mission Increasingly on the Agenda   88
IV. Evangelicals and Ecological Issues: A Rocha   92

Chapter 8: Sacred Space and Holy Places   94
I. The Significance of a Sabbatical in the Holy Land   94
II. Gloucester Diocese and Holy Places   96
III. The Church of South India and Holy Space   97
IV. The Impact of Covid Lockdown on Holy Space   98
V. Different Theological Responses to Sharing in Communion at Home during Lockdown   103

Chapter 9: The Local Parish Church Central to Church of England Ecclesiology   108
I. A Cambridge College Chapel Serving as a "Parish Church"   109
II. Gloucester Diocese and the Place of the Parish Church at the Heart of the Community   110
III. The Part Played by the Parish Church in My Own Upbringing   111
IV. Wycliffe College Missions and the Parish   112
V. A County-wide Event to Celebrate the New Millennium   113
VI. Parish-based Ministry in Semi-Retirement as a House for Duty Priest   115
VII. Parish Ministry and the Occasional Offices   118
VIII. Weddings Ministry   119
IX. The Church at the Heart of Village Life   121
X. National Debate in the Church of England About the Place of the Local Parish Church   122
XI. Changing Patterns of Ministry but Retaining Churches at the Heart of Village Life   125

Chapter 10: Reflections on the Impact of Covid Lockdown on Our Understanding and Practice of Church   **131**
   I. The Importance of Sacred Space   131
   II. Is It Important to Belong to a Local Church?   133
   III. Are Rural Churches More at Risk as a Result of the Pandemic?   133
   IV. Is the Future of the Parish Church Under Threat?   136

Chapter 11: Further Reflections on a Distinctive Anglican Ecclesiology   **141**
   I. Lambeth Conferences   141
   II. Reconciliation at the Heart of the Gospel   143
   III. A Focus on "Generous Orthodoxy"   145
   IV. Ordination Training: Course or College?   146
   V. A Dispersed Approach to Authority   149
   VI. Ordained Ministry: Catholic and Reformed   155
   VII. A Search for a "Pure" Church   157
   VIII. Comprehensiveness as a Characteristic of Anglican Theology   160
   IX. Trinitarian Theology as a Model for Unity in Diversity   164

Epilogue   **166**

Dedicated to my late wife, Rosemary, my soul mate and my best friend who inspired and challenged me by her Christian faith in the face of much suffering and was a wonderful partner in my ministry.

Preface

I have written this book for two main reasons. Firstly, I have come increasingly over my lifetime and ministry to value enormously the Anglican Church while standing within an Evangelical tradition and believing there is something very important to be found in holding together both an Evangelical tradition and the breadth and depth of the Anglican tradition. I have become aware that many Evangelical clergy especially those influenced by Charismatic renewal and those linked with Reform sit light to Anglican liturgy and operate with a Free Church gathered church ecclesiology rather than an ecclesiology focused on the parish church at the heart of the local community. Secondly, I have been concerned about the increasing tendency among bishops and at diocesan level to sideline the place of the parish which as I understand it has been at the heart of Church of England ecclesiology for many centuries and I have wanted to argue for retaining a focus on the importance of the local parish church.

I believe Anglican theology draws on Scripture but also on the riches of church tradition and also on personal experience and so, inevitably, in writing what I hope is a reasonably serious theological book interwoven with theology is my own life experience which has shaped my theology and spirituality over a lifetime.

I grew up in Brightlingsea in Essex. My father's family were very interested in the Theosophy movement and he kept a copy of the Upanishads by his bedside to read each night. My mother had been baptised as a baby but had not been confirmed and was not a regular churchgoer.

However, she prayed with me every night and sent me to afternoon Sunday School from an early age. Later on, I joined the church choir and was a server. At the age of 14 the headmaster of the Church of England Primary School stood down as church organist. I was attending the Guildhall School of Music each Saturday for piano lessons and had begun to learn the organ; the vicar encouraged me to become the church organist. He had trained as a singer at the Guildhall and trained the choir. My only experience of church life at this time was the Liberal Catholic tradition of Brightlingsea church though I did also occasionally attend area meetings of the Guild of the Servants of the Sanctuary.

Brightlingsea had two churches; the mediaeval church situated out of the town centre next to the historic manor house and a Victorian Chapel of Ease in the town centre. In the summer months Evensong was held in the mediaeval church. I have fond memories of enjoying worship, both the Sunday morning Eucharist and Evensong and sensing God's presence and love in the services.

Alongside Sunday worship from quite an early age I developed the practice of spending time each morning reading the Bible and praying. During my teenage years as I look back with the benefit of hindsight, I would describe myself as religious but there were areas of my life which were not compatible with a Christian lifestyle and I was aware of keeping God at arm's length as I didn't want him interfering in my life too much.

At 18 in my daily reading, I came to Acts 9 and the account of Paul's conversion. At the time I used the Authorised Version which included the words (not in the best manuscripts though found in the later account of Paul's conversion in Acts 26) "it is hard for you to kick against the pricks". As I read those words I realised I was *kicking against the pricks*, at the same time I had a strong sense of the risen Christ in the room with me assuring me of the depth of his love for me and assuring me that I needn't be afraid of letting go and allowing him to come and be right at the centre of my life, assuring me of his forgiveness of those areas of my life where I needed to be forgiven.

It seemed the natural thing to share my experience with my vicar. Unfortunately, rather than being supportive he dismissed the experience as purely psychological. However, shortly afterwards I went up to Cambridge to Corpus Christi College to read Classics. There I met, for the first time, people who described themselves as Evangelical and I found that they had experiences similar to my own; I became involved with CICCU (The Cambridge Inter-Collegiate Christian Union) but also attended College Chapel each Sunday and some mid-week services. I began to be aware of the different traditions within the Church of England.

Classics Part 1 is two years; during this period I had a growing sense of being called to ordination and was recommended for training at a national CACTM selection conference. So I switched to read Theology Part II also a two-year course. During my studies while many of my fellow students were moving from a conservative position to a more liberal stance influenced by their studies, I found myself moving in an increasingly conservative direction.

I had originally intended to stay on in Cambridge and train at Westcott House believing that it would be helpful to train in a college where most students would hold different theological views to my own. However, Maurice Wood, Principal of Oak Hill College, came and addressed a gathering of potential ordinands and I warmed to him as an inspirational leader and so ended up at Oak Hill for two years. In the meantime I had met up with Rosemary, the woman who was to become my wife who was a definite Evangelical. We met on a Children's Christian Holiday Club in the heart of Devon and were married at the end of my first year at Oak Hill. Over almost 55 years of married life she was my spiritual partner and partner in ministry and was a hugely significant person in my life including my spiritual life.

After Oak Hill I went on to serve a curacy at Emmanuel, Northwood, a Conservative Evangelical church. During this time looking back, I realise I sat light to Anglican tradition and ecclesiology and was influenced much more by what with the benefit of hindsight I would describe as a Free Church Evangelicalism.

Over the following years I served as a vicar of Holy Trinity, Margate, Vice-Principal of Wycliffe Hall in Oxford, Archdeacon of Surrey in Guildford diocese, then Bishop of Tewkesbury in Gloucester diocese and after retiring as a bishop I served as a House for Duty priest in a traditional Buckinghamshire group of village parishes and in retirement linked up together with my wife with a church in a Liberal Catholic tradition, but which in my view, helpfully holds together in a very Anglican way reflective biblical preaching and the centrality of the Eucharist. Over a life-time of discipleship and ministry in a variety of contexts I found myself coming to be increasingly appreciative of the Anglican tradition and wanting to hold together my Evangelical convictions and a strong commitment to all that is best in the Anglican tradition.

My prayer is that this book may play a part in encouraging Evangelicals (clergy and lay people) to be more appreciative of the Anglican tradition and to embrace it positively and in encouraging those in leadership in the church alongside a recognition of discovering new forms of church not to jettison the important place the parish church should occupy in local communities up and down the land.

John Went

Foreword One by the Right Revd Dr David Walker, Bishop of Manchester

This is a timely book. Reflecting on a life of following Jesus mostly as an adherent to the Evangelical tradition within the Church of England Bishop John Went not only tells his own story but the story of Anglican Evangelicalism here in England over the last half century and more. It was my privilege to be a colleague of John when we were suffragan bishops in neighbouring dioceses, and to benefit both from his wisdom and his passion for Christ.

It's a timely book because Church of England Evangelicals find themselves pulled in several directions at present, not least through tensions and divisions within the Evangelical constituency itself. Some of these have been brought to the fore by the Church's exploration of how to include LGBTQI+ within its fellowship. Others, and I would suggest that these are at least as important, come as a consequence of the discovery that many older senior Evangelical leaders had colluded in covering up the sexual abuse of young people being controlled by some of their most respected and revered colleagues. Finally, there are the divisions between those deeply committed to the local parish system and others who see it as largely outmoded, preferring a more network based understanding of Christian belonging.

John steps into this complex and conflicted field to offer us a clear articulation of an Evangelicalism that draws deeply from the wells of Anglican tradition, a tradition which he reminds us is not simply a child of the European Protestant Reformation but reaches behind that, building on its continuity with the Church of previous centuries. On these foundations, I believe that he has erected a model of firmly Anglican Evangelicalism, an ecclesiology where parishes, with their strong sense of the local community, provide the prime focus for mission and ministry and where bishops, and the diocesan structures behind them, provide the wider context and accountability.

It is not a vision that will appeal to all. As John remarks, there are many Evangelicals who at best are accidental Anglicans. They happen to worship in a Church of England parish because of geography or convenience. If they moved to another town or village, they might well worship as Baptists or in Independent churches. For others, not least some leaders, the idea of being held to account by any church structure beyond their own immediate zone of authority, is deeply unattractive.

Nevertheless. For those who wish to draw from the great resources of both the Evangelical and Anglican tradition, this book will provide much by way of nourishment and encouragement. My hope and prayer is that it will play its part in anchoring Anglican Evangelicals in their faith and their church belonging, through and beyond the challenges of the present day.

Foreword Two by the Right Revd Christopher Hill, retired Bishop of Guildford, former Co-Secretary of the Anglican-Roman Catholic International Commission and former President of the Council of European Churches

Bishop John Went's Apologia for a humane Evangelicalism should be read by anyone who cherishes the Evangelical and the Anglican tradition. Not least those who might be tempted to dub him a "back-slider". In earlier days after an Anglo-Catholic upbringing, he acknowledges coming to a living faith in Jesus but also a somewhat independent ecclesiology. He has since argued for a deeper Anglican ecclesiology which gives space for the experience of Christians as living members of the Body of Christ. All members of the Church are in St Paul's words "in Christ" and part of the community or communion of the Church. This experience means that doctrine is not static. Tradition is a living, changing experience. This does not mean anything goes because the *sensus fidelium* remains subject to Scripture. At the same time Scripture and Tradition require hermeneutic. Bishop John thus pleads for a generous orthodoxy which is expressed in an Anglican tradition of ordered liturgy composed of Word and Sacrament. The mission of the local parish must be to serve the whole community rather than become a gathered congregation of the elect. This will require a new evangelism of the Pilgrim Church, by definition far from static. After setting out this manifesto Bishop John expounds the detail chapter by chapter and deals with particular, sometimes contested issues. This courageous theological autobiographical account is highly relevant to contemporary Church of England Evangelicals and all Anglicans in a divided Communion.

Chapter 1

The Changing Face of Anglican Evangelicalism

A recent article in *The Spectator* raised the question of whether the Church of England needs Evangelicals. Theo Hobson writing in *The Spectator* is confident that the answer is a firm NO. He argues that "Evangelical dynamism cannot renew the Church as a whole. Its energy is too counter-cultural, it presents Christianity as an identity in sharp contrast to the surrounding culture. It insists that a true Christian is marked out by brave dissent from liberal views on sexual morality …. An Established Church cannot foreground such energy". In other words, an Established Church is not in a strong position to oppose the prevailing culture of the nation because its very existence is too intimately tied up with the life of the nation.

Carl R Trueman in an article written 13 April 2023 critiques the position of Hobson. He personally believes the Church should not be Established but his arguments in my view hold equally true for an Established Church. He argues that in the past the fault line in Western Christianity tended to run between the anti-supernatural and the supernatural. Did Jesus really heal the sick? Was the resurrection a real historical physical event? Today in his view the line is more subtle but equally important: Is there such a thing as human nature? The issue of the day he argues is anthropology. What does it mean to be human? Does being human mean that there is a moral framework to which I must conform, lest I dehumanise myself and others along with me? Traditional Christianity says yes; the modern world says no at least when it comes to sexual morality. Trueman argues that innovative views of sex, gender and marriage are inevitably repudiations of the fullness of Anglican tradition as "even the briefest glance at the Book of Common Prayer or the Homilies or the Thirty-Nine Articles will reveal".

I am clear in my own mind that the first Christians took a courageous stand against the prevailing morality in spite of being a tiny minority set over against the political might of the Roman Empire. Significantly by taking such a stand the long-term result was the "conversion" of the Roman Empire. In every generation there have been Christians who have had a significant impact on the culture of their day by refusing to conform to the prevailing view of society and taking their stand firmly on what they understood to be the teaching of Jesus and a wider biblical view.

The argument of my book drawing on my own life experience (a distinctively Anglican approach to theology) is that there are expressions of Evangelicalism which I would wish to distance myself from and that there is in my view a distinctively Anglican shaping of Evangelical faith. I am proud to count myself an Anglican and within the Anglican tradition to hold to an Evangelical understanding of my Christian faith. I write as someone who identifies both as a convinced Evangelical and at the same time as a convinced Anglican. Over a lifetime of discipleship and ministry I have remained greatly appreciative of all that the Evangelical tradition stands for. At the same time, I have come to value increasingly the riches found within the Anglican tradition. I believe that to be both Evangelical and Anglican, drawing on the riches of both traditions, marks me out from being an Evangelical in a Free Church tradition. During the years I have been privileged to exercise ministry in the Church of England as a curate, a parish priest, a vice-principal of a Theological College, an archdeacon, a bishop and a House for Duty priest I have been very aware of the changing face of both Evangelicalism and also of Anglicanism.

I am choosing to go into print at this particular time as I am aware from discussions in the wider Church of England that there is a real danger of the Church of England hierarchy moving significantly away from an understanding of Anglican ecclesiology that embraces a rich diversity of church traditions and has focused historically on the parish at the heart of her self-understanding. That ecclesiology has been in place since the Reformation and in the case of the parish structure can be traced back to the time of Archbishop Theodore in the seventh century. At the same time, I have witnessed many Evangelicals within the Church of England apparently identifying with a more Free Church Evangelical ecclesiology (something that was true of my own ecclesiological understanding early on in my discipleship and ministry) over against a distinctively Anglican ecclesiology shaped within an Evangelical tradition.

My own spiritual journey has taken place during this significant period of church history. I have become increasingly convinced that there is something distinctive worth identifying and affirming about being an Evangelical within an Anglican tradition. Looking back with the benefit of hindsight, I recognise that this conviction has been interwoven with my personal theological and spiritual journey over a lifetime. I plan to identify what I understand to be distinctive features of an Anglican ecclesiology from an Evangelical perspective and focus on those features to give shape to the book while at the same time drawing on ways in which my own spiritual and theological development has been interwoven with those features. I understand that a distinctive Anglican approach to theology, including ecclesiology, allows space for experience to play a part in shaping our understanding. I believe that by focusing on a distinctively Anglican Evangelical ecclesiology, Evangelicals within the Church of England and the wider Anglican Communion may be encouraged to reflect on their ecclesiological stance in the twenty-first century. I also dare to hope that some of the radical missionary thinking characterising the House of Bishops at this time might also be appropriately challenged. Interestingly in *The Telegraph* in late June 2023 there was an article reflecting on a debate to take place at the July General Synod on a recommendation by the Church Commissioners that rather than selling off non-viable parish churches and merging them with other parishes that these churches should be rented out for a limited period of time allowing for the parish church at a later date to reopen. This proposal has been warmly welcomed by the Revd Marcus Walker who is chairman of the "Save the Parish" campaign group and also a member of General Synod.

Do Church of England Evangelicals Stand in a Purely Reformed Tradition?

Reading again Tim Bradshaw's Latimer House Monograph (Latimer House is an Anglican Evangelical Research Centre based in Oxford within a Conservative Evangelical tradition): *The Olive Branch: An Evangelical Anglican Doctrine of the Church*, I found myself in agreement with much of the book's theses but also wish to argue that Tim Bradshaw does not give as much weight to a distinctively Anglican approach to evangelicalism as I would wish to.

Bradshaw covers an enormous breadth of theology including much ecumenical thought. He argues that for the Anglican Reformers the essential identity of the Church is Christological, rooted in the Person of Christ and in the preaching of the gospel. He draws on an impressive array of Reformers and contemporary writers from both Evangelical and also Anglo-Catholic sources and in addition from ecumenical documents to support his thesis. He cites Abraham as a key foundational person in identifying the people of God. He argues that such an understanding is worked out more fully in the writings of St Paul, especially in Romans and Galatians and finds expression in Article 18 of the Church of England 39 Articles: "The visible Church of Christ is a congregation of faithful men *[sic]*, in which the pure Word of God is preached and the sacraments duly administered."

Paul Minear in his book first published in 1960 *Images of the Church in the New Testament* manages to identify 96 different images! Many of them focus on the Church as community. Different denominations and different theological traditions have tended to focus on just one image or model as determinative for shaping their ecclesiology. One key model in the New Testament for the Church is **The Body of Christ** and this has featured as a key model historically and in many denominations. It is possible that St Paul's conversion experience shaped his understanding of the Church through this image. As the risen Christ confronted Saul on the Road to Damascus he asked why Saul was persecuting him. Saul was persecuting Christians but the clear implication in the question is that in persecuting Christians Saul was persecuting Christ; that there is an identification of Christ with his followers.

A similar understanding of the Church is found in St John's account of the Cleansing of the Temple. John unlike the Synoptic gospels sets this at the beginning of Jesus's ministry rather than in the final week of his life and so gives it a special emphasis in Jesus's self-understanding and understanding of the community of his followers. John portrays Jesus saying to the religious leaders "destroy this Temple and I will raise it up again in three days". They thought Jesus was referring to the literal Temple and saw it as an absurd claim, but John adds an editorial note that Jesus was referring to his resurrection body; the Church is identified with the risen body of Christ. Bradshaw argues that Anglo-Catholic tradition stresses that the Church is **in** Christ, the embodiment of Christ (a phrase often used is that the Church is an extension of the incarnation), while Evangelical ecclesiology stresses that Christ is present in the Church by his Spirit. Bradshaw writes: "The Church is not so much a form of Christ as the people of Christ in covenant with him."[1] In terms of loyalty to Scripture, I believe that there is New Testament support for both understandings of the relationship of Christ to his Church. A favourite two-word description of the life of the Christian and of the Church in the letters of St Paul is *in Christ*.

I grew up in Brightlingsea and from an early age attended the local parish church, serving, singing in the choir and from the age of 14 until I went to university being church organist. The vicar of the time would have described himself as Anglo-Catholic. At the time this was my only experience of Church. The main focus was on the sacramental life of the church. However, during my teens I developed the practice of reading my Bible each morning. As I was wending my way through the New Testament at the age of 18, I found myself reading the account of Paul's conversion in Acts 9. At the time I used the Authorised Version which includes the risen Christ saying to Saul "it is hard for you to kick against the pricks"; these words are not found in the best manuscript tradition in Acts 9 though they occur in the account of Paul's conversion in Acts 26. At the time though I was a very faithful church attender and would have described myself as very religious, there were several areas of my life where I was pretty determinedly keeping God at arm's length. Those words in the Authorised Version text of Acts 9 hit me hard; later on, I would understand this to have been a convicting work of the Holy Spirit. I sensed the presence of the risen Christ in the room with me and had a deep sense of God's love in Christ enfolding me. I also had a strong sense that because of God's amazing love, I need not be afraid of handing the control of my life over to the risen Christ. It was undoubtedly a significant moment in my Christian pilgrimage though I didn't fully understand its significance at the time. When I talked about the experience with my vicar he was unhelpfully dismissive viewing it in purely psychological rather than spiritual terms.

Many years later when I was Vice-Principal of Wycliffe Hall in Oxford, I found myself lecturing students on Church and

Ministry. Reading extensively in preparation for delivering these lectures I found myself inevitably reflecting deeply on my theological understanding of the nature of the Church. In my lectures I majored on the Church as a community gathered round the risen Christ, but explored different historical answers to the question: How is Christ encountered by the community of Christians? I recognised that Evangelicals in their answer to that question major especially on encountering Christ in the written Word. Anglo-Catholics have majored on encountering Christ through the ordained ministry and in the sacramental life of the Church. Charismatics have majored on the essential role played by the Holy Spirit in enabling us to encounter the risen Christ. Liberal traditions including Liberation theology have drawn on the Parable of the Sheep and Goats in Matthew 25 and have majored on encountering Christ as Christians serve the poor and needy. I came to acknowledge that the Anglican tradition seeks to hold these different traditions together, not seeing them as mutually exclusive but rather as complementary.

The Relationship of Scripture and Tradition

Another issue that Bradshaw addresses is the relationship between Scripture and Tradition in shaping our understanding of theology in general and ecclesiology in particular. John Henry Newman early on identified with an Evangelical understanding of Christian faith but ended up being welcomed into the Roman Catholic Church. Bradshaw critiques Newman in his opening chapter:

> [I]nstead of the long held Roman Catholic and Anglo-Catholic model of a church built on a solid rock of the foundational apostolic ministry and teaching, enshrined in the Bible and interpreted by the early creeds and councils, a church whose teaching and practice was *semper eadem*, always the same, Newman adopted the

model of a Spirit filled, living organism, growing through time. Whereas the old model stresses the fixity of faith and order, the new one stresses the inevitability of living development.[2]

Though I have a lot of sympathy with Bradshaw's position because of my own conviction as an Evangelical about the priority of Scripture for all, I wish as an Anglican Evangelical to make room for appropriate developments in history. I see biblical support for this in the promise of Jesus in John 16 that the Holy Spirit will lead us into all truth, not truth that is out of step with truth as found in the pages of Scripture yet enabling us to draw out truth as found in the pages of Scripture. Reflecting on Christian understanding through 2000 years of Christian history it seems self-evident to me that Christian doctrine has not remained static. Different interpretations of the faith once for all delivered have emerged at different times and in different cultural and social contexts.

One example would be the Christological statements drawn up by the early Councils reflecting on the New Testament witness to Christ as fully human while at the same time fully God as found supremely in John 1, 14 and John 1, 18 in the best manuscript reading: "the only-begotten God". The Church of the first four centuries drew quite heavily on Platonic philosophy in exploring both Christological and also Trinitarian theology. The early Fathers believed they were interpreting Scripture in drawing up Christological and Trinitarian statements, but they were interpreting Scripture through minds influenced significantly by Platonic philosophy, through the lens of Platonic philosophy.

An example drawn from more recent history would be the ordination of women as priests and bishops. I recognise that Evangelicals in the Church of England have adopted opposing views on this issue, but it would seem to me to be one area (a doctrinal area) where the Church has authority to look afresh at biblical testimony and come to a different view from our predecessors.

Another example from more recent history would be an understanding of Christian faith and experience shaped by the Pentecostalism of the twentieth century and Charismatic renewal which has characterised main line churches including the Roman Catholic Church. Pentecostal and Charismatic Christians have used the phrase "this is that"; in other words, the experience of the work of the Holy Spirit in their lives matches the experience of the first Christians as recorded in the Acts of the Apostles. Pentecostals and Charismatics have argued that the gifts of the Spirit which we find in 1 Corinthians 12 amongst other passages in the pages of the New Testament are available for Christians at every stage of Church history. Conservative Evangelicals have tended to take the view that the gifts were there to launch the Church and were not intended to be still available for every generation of Christians. The experience of Pentecostal and Charismatic Christians in recent history and in renewal movements at every stage of Christian history cannot easily be squared with such a view. The gifts of the Spirit have clearly not died out and are still available for Christians in every period of the history of the Church.

It is possible to draw on the Reformed tradition selectively in a way that affirms a more purely "Reformed" understanding of the Church. However, I believe that at the time of the Reformation that led to the existence of the Church of England the Reformers were clear that the Church of England while being Reformed was at the same time one with the undivided Church of the early centuries. Such a view finds expression especially in the writings of Hooker (to which I will return in a later chapter) often seen as "the Father of Anglicanism". It seems to me that though Bradshaw refers extensively to writers in an Anglo-Catholic tradition, he doesn't give sufficient weight to these Catholic strands in defining Anglicanism. He appears instead to use them to confirm his own Reformed Evangelical understanding of the nature of the Church.

During my time at Oak Hill Theological College preparing for ordination and during my curacy at Emmanuel Church, Northwood, I would have identified more closely with what I would describe with the benefit of hindsight as a Free Church Evangelical Ecclesiology. Over a lifetime of discipleship and ministry and in the light of a rich variety of life experiences, I have come to identify much more closely with a specifically Anglican perspective on my Evangelical faith that accepts the primacy of Scripture but is also prepared to acknowledge an appropriate place for tradition and experience in interpreting Scripture. I believe that there is a place for a distinctively Anglican approach to being an Evangelical and that this is significantly different from a purely Reformed understanding of Evangelical faith.

History of the term *Anglican*

The Latin term *Ecclesia Anglicana* can be traced back a long way to refer to the Church existing specifically in England. The phrase is found in the Magna Carta of 1215. It was used in its English form after the Reformation to stress that the Church of England had roots going back before the Reformation to earliest times and stood in continuity with the earliest expressions of the Christian faith. So far from being a new phenomenon emerging during the Reformation era it was one with the Church of the first centuries. I believe that the English Reformers were adamant that the Church of England was both Reformed and Catholic. Its distinctive character was shaped both over against what were seen as the errors of the Roman Catholic Church but also over against what were seen as the errors of the Puritans. It is of interest that Gladstone when as Prime Minister he was defending the validity of Anglican Orders (something denied by the Roman Catholic Church explicitly in Pope Leo XIII's papal encyclical of 1896 which described Anglican Orders as "absolutely null and void") in his *Church Principles* of 1840 used the term Anglican to describe the Church of England over against the Roman Catholic Church.

Anglicans I believe are entitled to lay claim to the word "Catholic", from two Greek words translated literally as "throughout the whole" i.e., universal, an affirmation about the Church in the Nicene Creed which Anglican Christians affirm every Sunday in their worship. I confess to finding it slightly irritating when I drive past Roman Catholic Churches here in London where my wife and I came to live in retirement and the Church board confidently describes the Church as "Catholic" omitting the word "Roman"!

Gladstone used the term Anglican to refer to the Church of England. During the nineteenth century the term Anglican Communion came to be used to refer to a widespread group of churches in communion with the Church of England through being in communion with the Archbishop of Canterbury. In 1867 the first Lambeth Conference took place as a forum for fellowship and study and seeking to hold together in unity a broad spectrum of churches across the world. It was called by Archbishop Longley in the light of issues raised by the publication of Essays and Reviews in 1860 which challenged traditional views of the authority of Scripture and issues raised by the "unorthodox" views of Colenso Bishop of Natal about the Pentateuch. From the start it was clear that any resolutions passed by the Lambeth Conference did not have the authority of papal encyclicals but were simply an attempt to give expression to views seen as expressive of Anglicanism and to seek to hold diverse churches together in some kind of unity. Again, I shall return to issues relating to the Anglican Communion and its rich diversity held somehow together in unity in subsequent chapters.

Characteristics of Anglican Theology

Two phrases are frequently used in relation to Anglicanism: one is *dispersed authority* and the other is a *comprehensive church*, holding alongside each other views which in other denominations would be understood as contradictory and mutually exclusive but in the Anglican tradition are seen as potentially complementary. I shall be returning to these themes in subsequent chapters, but at this point I am flagging up that I believe these two phrases characterise a distinctively Anglican approach and are held by me alongside my strongly held Evangelical convictions and play an important part in shaping my Evangelical convictions.

Sola Scriptura was a watch word of the Reformation and many Evangelicals have taken that as excluding all other sources for our understanding of Christian truth but that does not seem to me to be the position adopted by the Anglican Church. Another way of understanding *Sola Scriptura* is to see it as referring to the basis of our salvation; that our understanding of the grounds for being saved is to be found in Scripture and Scripture alone. Similarly, when reference is made to "the plain sense of Scripture" that is not an all-embracing term implying that we can find answers to all issues and questions simply by reading them off the pages of the Bible, but rather that the Bible is crystal clear about how a person can discover and enjoy a relationship with God, the basis of our salvation. It leaves the door open to wrestling with issues of interpretation on a host of issues where the Bible is far from conveying a plain sense. So Christians can disagree and have disagreed over the practice of baptism (Infant or Believers Baptism) and over the gifts of the Holy Spirit and over the ministry of women in the church to take just three examples.

A favourite passage for Evangelicals about the authority of Scripture (and one frequently quoted by myself over the years in ministry) is found in St Paul's second letter to

Timothy chapter 3 verses 16–17. As often, the Greek is open to more than one translation. I quote the New International Version (NIV) translation: "All Scripture is God-breathed and is useful for teaching, rebuking, correcting and training in righteousness, so that the servant of God may be thoroughly equipped for every good work." Some versions simply describe all Scripture as inspired by God; that opens the door to a variety of views of inspiration. I might refer to Handel's *Messiah* as inspired or Schubert's ninth symphony as inspired. God-breathed following the NIV translation (the Greek is literally God-breathed) offers a rather more unique and authoritative interpretation of inspired. Comparisons can be drawn with the breath of God and the spoken word of God in the creation narrative in Genesis 1 and 2. As an Evangelical I would wish to invest Scripture with a very high, indeed unique, view of inspiration that attributes unique authority to the Word of God. However, the main focus for that inspired Word of God is to equip us as Christians for "every good work" and "training in righteousness". It is an intended practical outcome of Godly living.

In the case of Infant Baptism, Tradition helpfully plays a part for Anglicans. As an Anglican Evangelical I am persuaded that on balance there is both a biblical case (in terms of Covenant theology) and a New Testament case (household baptisms) for Infant Baptism but not a totally conclusive case. Reading the Acts of the Apostles on its own, I would have to acknowledge that there is more evidence for Believers Baptism. However, I also recognise that there is abundant evidence of Infant Baptism from earliest times in the practice of the Church as explored by Joachim Jeremias in his *Infant Baptism in the first four centuries*, the place of Tradition complementing the evidence of Scripture and shaping our interpretation of the biblical evidence. It is of interest that a number of my fellow students at Oak Hill Theological College left the Church of England ministry within five years of being ordained because they were unable to accept that Infant Baptism had biblical support.

As far as gifts of the Holy Spirit are concerned, I would as an Anglican Evangelical hold together both the evidence of the New Testament and the experience of Charismatic Christians in the Church of England (and the wider Anglican Communion) from the second half of the twentieth century alongside giving appropriate weight to the experience of Pentecostal Christians and the experience of African-American Christians in the Azusa Street Revival that took place from 1906. As already mentioned, Pentecostal and Charismatic Christians argue that "this is that", namely that their experience of the Holy Spirit is equivalent to the experience of the first Christians as recorded in the Acts of the Apostles and as promised by Jesus to his followers "you will be baptised in the Holy Spirit". The Anglican inclusion of experience and the *consensus fidelium* (the consensus of the faithful) would support such an approach to belief about the place of the Holy Spirit in the community of faith.

As an Anglican whose faith and Christian convictions and experience have been shaped by Evangelical doctrine and experience, I am clear that Tradition and Experience and the *consensus fidelium* have to be subordinate to the testimony of Scripture. As Tradition evolved within the developing life of the Church some paths can be accepted as in line with the testimony of Scripture while other paths moved in a direction that was not consistent with Scripture.

Any survey of the Anglican Communion would reveal a rich breadth of theological views and understandings: Evangelical, Catholic, Charismatic (an extremely significant movement during the latter half of the twentieth century, reflected in Charismatic songs in a very wide cross-section of churches that wouldn't identify themselves as Charismatic but value gentle Charismatic worship), Liberal. Within each of these broad headings there are a variety of nuanced interpretations. So within my own Evangelical tradition during my lifetime as a priest there have been significant developments. When I was ordained in 1969 to a curacy in a Conservative Evangelical church (Emmanuel, Northwood, with David Bubbers as my training incumbent who went on to be General Secretary of the Church Pastoral Aid Society and I had the privilege of my final year as a curate being with Richard Bewes as my training incumbent who went on to be Rector of All Souls Langham Place, a leading Conservative Evangelical Church), having trained at Oak Hill Theological College, Evangelicals at that time were essentially divided between Conservative or Liberal who were viewed by Conservative Evangelicals as not "true" Evangelicals. Today I would identify many different strands within Anglican Evangelicalism: Sacramental Evangelicals, Charismatic Evangelicals, anti-Charismatic Evangelicals (some of our students at Wycliffe Hall during my time as Vice-Principal in the 1980s argued that you couldn't call yourself Evangelical if you were a Charismatic Christian), Radical Evangelicals, Open Evangelicals. There are probably other nuanced approaches which I haven't identified. In a later chapter I shall explore a term that has increasingly characterised some Anglican Evangelicals, myself included, that was used by Brian McLaren at an evening session at the 2008 Lambeth Conference, namely *Generous Orthodoxy*.

Trinitarian theology has also been a characteristic of Anglican theology to which I shall return in a later chapter, and I believe that an understanding of the nature of the Trinity as three persons but one Godhead helpfully draws us to an understanding of the Church as giving expression to unity in diversity and diversity in unity.

Another characteristic of Anglican theology is making space for a significant role of the words and forms of worship (our Liturgy) in shaping our theology. The genius of Cranmer was to design services that in addition to the systematic reading of Scripture (the Old Testament once a year, the New Testament twice in the year, the Psalms on a monthly basis) was characterised by numerous Scriptural references and allusions. The introduction of new services from the 1960s onwards inevitably raised questions about whether the Church of England's theology was being significantly changed subtly by the introduction of these new services. For example, was eucharistic theology changing from the understanding of the Reformers, especially Cranmer? As an Anglican might I wish to embrace these changes while as an Evangelical might I wish to resist such changes?

Also, Anglican theology has been characterised by the holding together as equally significant for our Christian discipleship Word and Sacrament. Again, this characteristic will be explored more fully in a subsequent chapter.

A characteristic of Anglican polity is a focus on the local parish as at the heart of Anglican ecclesiology. As mentioned earlier the parish system has an extremely long history having been introduced by Archbishop Theodore in the seventh century. Clearly the social and cultural factors at that time were significantly different from England in the twenty-first century. Inevitably many question the relevance of the parish system in our contemporary setting but my own conviction is that the vision of a parish church at the heart of every community serving the needs of that community, seeking opportunities to share the gospel with those living in that community is an important characteristic of Anglican church life and still relevant in the twenty-first century.

As well as changes in Anglican theology and self-understanding down the centuries since the Reformation, Evangelical thinking has not remained static. One key area which I shall wish to explore more fully in a subsequent chapter is Evangelical understanding of Mission.

Another area of change for many within an Evangelical tradition has been our understanding of biblical interpretation. This has proved controversial within Evangelical circles and some Evangelicals have seen the acknowledgement of the place of hermeneutics (interpretation) in our application of Scripture to contemporary issues as a serious mistake damaging to the integrity and historical Evangelical approach to Scripture. As already mentioned, this touches on the Reformation watchword of *sola scriptura* which clashes with the Anglican emphasis on three (or four) strands to the formation of Anglican doctrine, namely Scripture, Tradition (including *consensus fidelium*), Reason (with Experience as either in addition to Reason or included under the umbrella of Reason).

An increasingly popular image of understanding Christian discipleship in the contemporary Church is **Pilgrimage**. The great thing about pilgrimage is that it embraces journeying rather than remaining static in the same place. I have personally found this image helpful for my own spiritual life. Inevitably this raises a question about whether in embracing this journey I have moved away from convictions that once were important to me as an Evangelical and whether I have taken on board convictions that at one time I would have been suspicious of as not compatible with my Evangelical convictions. In my early days as Bishop of Tewkesbury I was asked by my diocesan bishop to visit a parish priest in his 90s to persuade him that it was time for him to retire! He was one of the few remaining clergy in Gloucester diocese at the time appointed before the introduction of a retirement age and had the freehold which allowed him to remain in office until his death. He had worked in North Africa as a missionary among Muslims before becoming a parish priest in Gloucester diocese. He was totally committed to the Authorised Version of the Bible and the 1662 Prayer Book. He attracted a reasonable number of people drawn from a wide geographical area who valued his approach. His first wife had died and he had married a much younger woman who printed his sermons weekly and distributed them. In my conversation with him he challenged me over whether I was a "back-slider" and had abandoned the Evangelical convictions which I had embraced during my time at Cambridge and my involvement with CICCU (The Cambridge Inter-Collegiate Christian Union). His probing questions did lead me to engage in some serious soul-searching over a few weeks, but I remained convinced that my faithfulness as a disciple and as a minister of the gospel had rightly moved in new directions. Interestingly, I failed to convince him that he needed to retire. Later, the archdeacon persuaded him by arguing that it would be helpful to his young wife if he had settled her in his retirement home while he was still alive! He died shortly after moving with his young wife into a retirement home provided by the Church of England Pension Board!

My argument in this book is that Anglican theology and self-understanding have not remained static since the Reformation and neither have Evangelical theology and self-understanding stood still over the years and that as a convinced Anglican Evangelical, I have wished to embrace many of the fresh insights and developments that have characterised both Anglican thought and Evangelical thought during my lifetime and in earlier decades.

In Chapter 2 I explore the central place of the Bible both in Anglicanism and in Evangelical theology. In Chapter 3 I focus on holding together Word and Sacrament as an Anglican Evangelical. In Chapter 4 I explore the Anglican emphasis on Prayer and Liturgy shaping our beliefs as Christians. Chapter 5 explores the challenge of hermeneutics and the impact of Ecumenical relationships on Evangelical thought. In Chapter 6 I major on the centrality of Evangelism as a key characteristic of Evangelicals and the gospel as cross-shaped but then in Chapter 7, I reflect on the move among Evangelicals (and key

Anglican theology) to understand Mission on a very broad canvas. Chapter 8 is dedicated to reflecting on Sacred Space as a distinctively Anglican understanding of Church. Chapter 9 explores the local parish church as central to traditional Church of England ecclesiology traced back to the seventh century. In Chapter 10 I reflect on the impact of Covid lockdown on our understanding and practice of Church. Chapter 11 as a concluding chapter includes further reflections on a distinctive Anglican Ecclesiology including reflections on the two Lambeth Conferences I was privileged to attend as Bishop of Tewkesbury in 1998 when George Carey was Archbishop of Canterbury and in 2008 when Rowan Williams was Archbishop of Canterbury.

Chapter 2

The Central Place of the Bible in Anglicanism and Evangelical Theology

The Place of the Bible in the Reformation and Pre-Reformation Trailblazers

The Church of England Ordination Service at the time of the Reformation made a very clear statement about a very different understanding of the focus of ordained ministry. In the Roman Catholic ordinal, instruments given to the newly ordained priest consisted of a chalice and ciborium. These made a clear statement about the focus of ordained ministry, sacramental with an emphasis on the Eucharist (the Mass). These were replaced with the giving of a Bible. This conveyed an equally clear message that the focus of ordained ministry was seen to be a ministry of the Word, a preaching ministry.

John Wycliffe was a significant forerunner of the Reformation. He came to believe that the Bible was central to understanding Christian faith and living out the Christian life. At the time the Bible was only available in the Latin version that had been translated by St Jerome from the Hebrew and Greek. Ordinary lay people had no access therefore to the words of Scripture but were totally dependent on the priest. Wycliffe was determined that the Bible should be available to ordinary lay Christians in a format that they could understand. From 1380–1381 he was busy in his rooms in Queens College, Oxford, working to produce a translation of the Bible into English.

Another key figure preceding the Reformation was Tyndale. Born in Gloucestershire he studied at Oxford university and became convinced that the Bible and the Bible alone should determine Christian belief and practice. In 1523 he began work on translating the New Testament from Luther's German translation. He subsequently began work on translating the Old Testament but was martyred before he completed his translation. Like Wycliffe he was convinced that ordinary lay Christians should be able to read the Bible in their own language.

A significant additional factor at the time historically was that books had been made much more accessible to ordinary people as a result of William Caxton inventing the printing press in 1476 and becoming the first English retailer of printed books. Certainly by 1500 and probably as early as 1200, the majority of the population were familiar with reading though only a small percentage could write. By 1500 it is estimated that almost everyone would at least know someone who could read. Between 1100 and 1500 the ability to read moved from the sphere of the monastery, the church and the university to family life. The availability of printed books together with the translation of the Bible into English meant a significant percentage of the population for the first time had access to the Bible for themselves rather than being totally dependent on the clergy.

Interestingly, there has been a significant further development in my lifetime through social media. I still am a proud owner of a decent library and love to be able to have access to books, but I am aware that my grandchildren are much more likely to search the world-wide web and communicate through social media. This presents fresh challenges to the church in seeking to communicate the gospel in our twenty-first-century Western world. End of a short digression! I return to the place of the Bible in both the Anglican tradition and among Evangelicals.

The 39 Articles are a clear statement about key beliefs held by the Church of England Reformers. Article 6 is very clear about the central place to be held by the Bible in determining Christian belief: "Holy Scripture containeth all things necessary for salvation: so that whatsoever is not contained therein, nor may be proved thereby is not to be required of any man that it should be believed as an article of faith or be thought requisite or necessary to salvation." In my opening chapter I mentioned *Sola Scriptura* as a watchword of the Reformers. However, the Anglican Reformers alongside a strong emphasis on the church being reformed in the light of scripture also argued that the church was one with the universal (Catholic) church of the early centuries. In the developing Anglican tradition as finding expression, for example, in the writings of Hooker, often referred to as "the Father of Anglicanism", there is reference to a three-fold cord of Scripture, Tradition and Reason (and within Reason Experience). So *Sola Scriptura* in my opinion has to be understood within Anglicanism rather differently from within a more Free Church Evangelical tradition.

Various Factors in the Anglican Tradition Influence the Interpretation of the Bible

In a later chapter I shall make reference to the Lambeth Conferences. At the 1948 Lambeth Conference the Bishops drafted a statement about the distinctive nature of authority within Anglicanism:

> Authority, as inherited by the Anglican Communion from the undivided Church of the early centuries of the Christian era, is single in that it is derived from a single divine source, and reflects within itself the richness and historicity of the Divine Revelation, the authority of the eternal Father, the incarnate Son and the life-giving Spirit. It is distributed among Scripture, Tradition, Creeds, the Ministry of the Word and Sacraments, the witness of saints and consensus fidelium, which is the continuing experience of the Holy Spirit through the faithful people in the Church.[3]

The key phrase that is used to summarise this approach to authority is **dispersed authority**. As an Evangelical I believe in the ultimate final authority of Scripture, but as an Anglican I accept that Scripture is interpreted through a distinctive lens that embraces Tradition, Reason, Experience, so Scripture doesn't stand alone. In a later chapter I shall explore the important issue of **Hermeneutics**, the process involved in interpreting Scripture at different historical times and in different cultural contexts. Such an approach gravitates against a static once for all statement of Christian belief and practice but allows for development and change, always ultimately subject to being consistent with the testimony of Scripture.

The Evangelical Revival, and the Bible and Preaching Ministry

In the eighteenth century the Church of England was at quite a low ebb spiritually; it was thought in some areas that most of the bishops were Deists rather than Trinitarian Theists. During the eighteenth century there was a significant Evangelical awakening. In 1738 Charles and John Wesley had Evangelical conversions. About the same time Handel's *Messiah* was sung for the first time, powerfully conveying the good news of salvation foretold in the Old Testament prophets and finding fulfilment in the birth, life, death and resurrection of Jesus Christ. I personally find listening to Handel's *Messiah* a deeply spiritual experience and on one occasion while on the staff of Wycliffe Hall chose to go on Good Friday to hear *Messiah* in the Festival Hall; it was as spiritually enriching as attending a three hours at the cross service.

In 1759 Charles Simeon was born who was to become a very significant figure in the Evangelical revival that took place in the late eighteenth and early nineteenth centuries, though in his early days at university he was far from being a shining example of Christian faith. He was born into an aristocratic family; after being educated at Eton College in 1779 he went up to Kings College, Cambridge; at that time his main interests were horses, fashion and gambling. However, he was told that he must receive Holy Communion on Easter Sunday and preparing to receive took him on a spiritual journey that resulted in his conversion. He wrote in his diary "On the Wednesday of Holy Week began a hope of mercy. On the Thursday, that hope increased. On ... Easter Day... I awoke with these words upon my heart and lips Jesus Christ is risen today, halleluia, halleluia!" He went on to be ordained and in 1782 he was appointed Vicar of Holy Trinity, Cambridge, where he remained for the rest of his life exercising an extraordinary influence within the Church of England.

His appointment was not welcomed by most at Holy Trinity who had wanted another vicar; the rented pews of the wealthy at that time were locked so congregation members had to stand in the aisles. As time passed Simeon attracted an increasing number of students who welcomed his clear Evangelical preaching. At the time of his death in 1836 it was estimated that one third of all Church of England ministers had been influenced by his preaching and teaching. In addition to his ministry in Cambridge, he exercised a wider influence playing a part in the formation of several Evangelical Missionary societies and also in founding the Simeon Trust which bought up the patronage of many churches up and down the country, and so was able to appoint Evangelical clergy to those livings, thus influencing the ethos of the Church of England right up to the present time. Gladstone reflected on the influence of Simeon describing him as responsible for "a real and profound revival of the spiritual life".[4]

The Bible was central to Simeon's faith and he was deeply committed to biblical preaching in what came to be known as an expository style of preaching, which is essentially breaking open the text (either a single verse or a passage) and exploring its meaning for the assembled congregation and applying it to contemporary Christian discipleship. I have already referred to a significant change at the time of the Reformation in understanding the focus of ordained ministry expressed in the ordination service by replacing the giving of a chalice and ciborium to the newly ordained with the giving of a Bible. For Simeon the heart of his ministry was preaching and encouraging students in small groups and on a one-to-one basis to engage with Scripture. Though Simeon encouraged people to put the Bible at the heart of their spiritual life he was also a committed Anglican, deeply committed to the Book of Common Prayer.

In addition to Simeon there were other significant individuals who played an important part in shaping the Church of England in an Evangelical direction through preaching ministry and through founding Evangelical movements. Edward Bickersteth who was for a time General Secretary of the Church Missionary Society and founded the Evangelical Alliance delighted in preaching hour and half-long sermons. He was part of a large clerical family; his son, also Edward, was Bishop of Exeter, a nephew was Dean of Lichfield, a grandson, also Edward, founded the Cambridge Mission to Delhi and was later Bishop of South Tokyo.

Other influential Evangelicals were members of the Venn family. John Venn, son of Henry Venn, was Vicar of Holy Trinity, Clapham, and founded the Clapham Sect that included people like William Wilberforce; they played a significant role in the abolition of slavery. Though Evangelicals have sometimes been accused of being so heavenly minded that they are no earthly use, members of the Clapham Sect testify to a strong social conscience and a commitment to see the world transformed and to understand mission in much broader terms than purely personal evangelism. I shall be returning to this issue in a later chapter.

As an Evangelical the Bible has played a key role in my own spiritual journey. I hadn't heard of Evangelicals as I grew up in

Brightlingsea in Essex. My parents sent me to afternoon Sunday School at an early age and later I joined the Church Choir and was a server. At the age of 14 when the then organist stood down, I became organist for four years before going up to Cambridge. The tradition of the Church was Liberal Catholic and that at the time was my only experience of Church life and Christian experience. The focus of Church life was the Eucharist; I would serve at an 8.00 a.m. service and then attend the main morning service of Holy Communion and Evensong. However, though Communion was the main focus of my experience of church life I read my Bible each morning and set aside time for prayer. I would have described myself at the time as very religious. However, looking back with the benefit of hindsight, I was aware that there were areas of my life where I was determined to keep God at arm's length.

As mentioned in my introductory chapter at the age of 18 I came in my reading of the New Testament to the account of Saul's conversion in Acts 9. At the time I was using the Authorised Version which includes the phrase (not in the best manuscript readings though in the later account in Acts 26 of Saul's conversion) "it is hard for you to kick against the pricks". As I read those words the Holy Spirit pricked my conscience; I had an overwhelming sense of the risen Christ in the room with me and of his all-embracing love and a strong sense that I need not be afraid of allowing Christ to come into every area of my life, that because of his amazing love I could safely entrust my life fully to him.

I talked with my vicar about this experience and sadly he was less than helpful, explaining it away in purely psychological terms and suggesting it might be helpful for me to have a session with a psychiatrist. It was only when I went up a few months later to study Classics at Cambridge that I met with Evangelical Christians who talked of similar spiritual experiences, and I became involved with the Cambridge Inter-Collegiate Christian Union (CICCU).

Because the Bible has been central to my Christian faith, I was keen early on to be able to read the Old and New Testaments in their original languages. Having read Classics Part 1 at Cambridge reading the New Testament, though the Koine Greek of the New Testament is different from Classical Greek in a number of areas, in Greek has always been relatively straightforward and it is my practice to use my Greek testament each day for my daily reading.

When I moved from Classics Part I to Theology Part II at Cambridge, I had a number of options and chose to take the Philosophy option rather than Hebrew. However, later at Theological College I was able to learn Hebrew with the Vice-Principal, John Taylor, later Bishop of St Albans. Keeping my Hebrew up has proved more challenging, but I read a psalm in Hebrew each morning and take an Old Testament book regularly and read it in the Hebrew using a commentary based on the Hebrew text. I find it immensely helpful to be able to read the Bible in its original languages and often find treasures which would have been passed by if reading in an English translation.

Because the Bible played a significant role in my discovering a living Christian faith, the Bible throughout my life has continued to be very significant in nurturing my spiritual life and expository preaching has been a very important part of my ministry, seeing the heart of my ordained ministry as that of a Pastor-Teacher. However, in later chapters I will explore different models of preaching, some of which I came to view as more Anglican than purely Evangelical and I will explore how I shifted from a focus almost exclusively on the Bible and preaching to a recognition of the importance of holding together Word and Sacrament as a distinctively Anglican form of my Evangelical faith and ministry.

In this Chapter I have sought to argue that the Bible is central to a Reformed understanding of Christian faith and was crucial to the Church of England Reformation and also central to a distinctively Evangelical understanding of Church and Ministry and of personal faith. However, I have also hinted that there is a distinctively Anglican Evangelical approach to the place of the Bible in the life of the Church and in Christian discipleship and to preaching.

Chapter 3

An Anglican Evangelical Holding Together Word and Sacrament

A favourite Easter story for me has always been the Emmaus Road recorded in Luke 24. Two individuals, Cleopas and his travelling companion, possibly his wife, on the first Easter Sunday are walking from Jerusalem to Emmaus. Sadly no one is quite sure where Emmaus was and there are three sites that seek to lay claim to be the place. The couple are engaged in vigorous discussion; the Greek word used by Luke suggests bouncing ideas backwards and forwards in an argumentative way. Maybe one of them is inclined to believe the report that the women who visited the tomb early Easter morning had brought of the body of Jesus no longer being in the tomb, and of having seen a vision of angels who declared that he was alive, while the other one refuses to believe their report, dismissing it as an old wives' tale. A stranger joins them and ends up giving an amazing detailed exposition of the Old Testament scriptures referring to the Messiah. As they approach their journey's end, they persuade the Stranger to join them for a meal. As they sit at table the Stranger takes bread, blesses it and shares it with them. Then Luke comments that their eyes were opened to recognise the Stranger to be no other than the risen Lord.

It is interesting to reflect on how the two travellers recognised Jesus. Many have assumed that as he took the bread and broke it and gave it to them they saw the nail prints in his hands. That may have been so. However, I like the suggestion of Trevor Dennis in *The Easter Stories* that what caused them to recognise him as the risen Lord was the fact that he took on two very different roles, one of host, who would pray a blessing over the bread and one of a servant who would break the bread and distribute it to the guests. Who did they know who though he shared the divine nature, assumed the role of a servant/slave? Their minds may well have gone back to the last meal shared by Jesus when he took a bowl of water and a towel and washed his disciples' feet one by one, the act of a humble servant and they may well have heard about that act of selfless service.[5]

But there is more in this wonderful story; significantly as they look back on their journey and reflect on the way the Stranger had opened up the Scriptures for them as they walked together they recognised that their hearts had been on fire in response to the breaking open of the Old Testament Scriptures and realising how Jesus as Messiah was found in verse after verse and passage after passage of those Scriptures.

For me this offers a convincing biblical support for holding together Word and Sacrament, sharing in a eucharistic meal and opening up the Scriptures through expository preaching, in a way that is faithful to an Anglican tradition.

Eucharistic or Non-Eucharistic Interpretation of the Emmaus Road Story and John 6?

I see this as a very Anglican story of Word and Sacrament held together. However, I need to mention that not all scholars see references to the Breaking of Bread in Luke-Acts as referring to early celebrations of the Eucharist. Graham H Twelftree in *People of the Spirit: Exploring Luke's View of the Church* (SPCK 2009) argues that the references to breaking bread in Luke are purely references to sharing ordinary meals and that we are incorrect to see in them sacramental references to early celebrations of the Eucharist. My own view is that we are right to see in these passages a reference to the meals that the early Christians shared in memory specifically of the last meal Jesus shared with his disciples when he took bread, broke it and shared it with the disciples and shared a cup of wine with them, investing in the bread and the cup a spiritual significance related to his forthcoming death on the cross. It is true that Jesus shared many meals with his disciples during the three years of his public ministry (in fact Luke's gospel is structured round eight meals Jesus shared in and each of them an occasion for teaching), but I am convinced that the last meal he shared with them must have held a very special place in their collective memory and carried special significance. According to the Synoptic gospels it was a Passover meal with imagery drawn from the Exodus informing Jesus's own interpretation of his approaching death on the cross. My own interpretation of the Emmaus Road over against Twelftree's approach is a reminder of the difficulty of focusing on the "plain sense" of Scripture which doesn't allow for differences of interpretation. Again, this is an issue to which I will be returning later in the book.

One of my colleagues when I was on the staff of Wycliffe Hall saw John's gospel as anti-sacramental and no eucharistic overtones in John 6 and the account of the Feeding of the 5000 followed by an extended reflection by Jesus according to John on the significance of the meal. The use of the four verbs: *take, break, bless, distribute* very early on in the developing history of the Church came to refer to the four key actions at the heart of the Church's celebration of the Eucharist. I personally cannot fail to see references in Luke-Acts to meals shared with the risen Christ and the references in John 6 to eating Christ's flesh and drinking his blood as referring to celebrations of the Eucharist by the first generation of Christians. Rather than seeing John as anti-sacramental, I see him as deeply sacramental.

Again, the way John writes up the extended theological reflection by Jesus in the wake of the Feeding of the 5000 in my view holds together both Word and Sacrament. In vv53–56 of John 6 there is some very strong literal language used:

Very truly I tell you, unless you eat the flesh of the Son of Man and drink his blood, you have no life in you.

Whoever eats my flesh and drinks my blood has eternal life and I will raise them up on the last day. For my flesh is real food and my blood is real drink. Whoever eats my flesh and drinks my blood remains in me and I in them.

However, when some of the wider group of disciples take issue with this very literal language John represents Jesus going on to say (v63): "The Spirit gives life; the flesh counts for nothing. The words I have spoken to you – they are full of the Spirit and life." Then in v67 when Jesus asks the 12 whether they also wish to leave Peter speaks up on behalf of the 12: "Lord, to whom shall we go? You have the words of eternal life." As with the powerful Emmaus Road account, Word and Sacrament in my view are held together here in John 6 and Jesus's extended reflection on the significance of the Feeding of the 5000.

From my days growing up in a Liberal Catholic Anglican Church I was nurtured Sunday by Sunday by sharing in the Eucharist, but in my personal spiritual life day by day, I was more nurtured by reading the Bible. Both Word and Sacrament played a part in my spiritual formation and that continued through my time at Cambridge and involvement with the college chapel and the weekly Sunday morning Eucharist alongside sharing in personal Bible study and meeting with other Christians through CICCU to study the Bible.

In my curacy at Emmanuel Church, Northwood, a Conservative Evangelical church, the focus was much more on the preaching ministry. Many congregation members were content simply to share in the Eucharist (their preferred names for that service would have been Holy Communion or The Lord's Supper) once a month or even less frequently. Their spiritual life was above all nurtured by personal Bible study, group Bible study and the preaching ministry.

Keele Congress and Anglican Evangelicals' Placing More Emphasis on the Eucharist at the Centre of Sunday Worship

I have already mentioned that Anglican self-understanding has not remained static down the years and the same is true of Evangelicalism. During my own lifetime and ministry, there have been significant changes in Evangelical self-understanding. In 1967 1000 Evangelical delegates (almost entirely half and half clergy and lay people) plus observers from the Roman Catholic and Orthodox Churches and from the Free Churches met at the university of Keele. Amongst other recommendations Keele acknowledged that the Eucharist should be the main weekly act of worship. In the wider church in the 1950s, the Parish Communion movement had made considerable headway arguing for the Lord's Service on the Lord's Day. In many churches Matins was phased out and increasingly Evening services became far less well attended. Significantly, at Keele Evangelicals in the Church of England acknowledged that their worship should be focused much more on the Eucharist. After all Wesley as an Evangelical referred to Holy Communion as *a converting ordinance.*

During my own lifetime among some Evangelicals, there has been a willingness to be open to a measure of truth in understandings of the Eucharist that traditionally have only been associated with Anglo-Catholic views. Christopher Cocksworth, Bishop of Coventry, in his PhD on "Evangelical Eucharistic Thought in the Church of England" offers evidence for Eucharistic practice being more central among Church of England Evangelicals historically than often assumed, and also an openness to insights from more Catholic views of eucharistic Presence and even eucharistic Sacrifice. The conclusions Cocksworth reaches in his book have come to be shared by an increasing number of Anglican Evangelicals.

During my time as Vicar of Holy Trinity, Margate, (1975–1983), I came to value the Eucharist increasingly and organised our four Sunday services in such a way that in addition to a weekly Prayer Book Communion service at 8.00 a.m. there was Communion at one of the other three main services on a weekly basis. When I arrived at Holy Trinity in 1975, I found that my predecessor hadn't included a short sermon at the 8.00 a.m. service of Holy Communion. At Emmanuel, Northwood, where I had served my curacy we always had a short sermon at the 8.00 a.m. service and for me it was important that Word and Sacrament went together, so on my first Sunday I introduced a short address. At the door of the church at the end of the service one of the local Undertakers (we later became firm friends!) said to me: "I come to this service to have a sense of meeting with God and not to have my thoughts interrupted by you preaching a sermon!" This was just one of several "battles" I needed to be engaged in as I sought to take the Church in a more clearly Evangelical direction than my predecessor. At this stage in my ministry, however, I probably identified more closely with a Free-Church Evangelical tradition, though during my eight and half years at Holy Trinity for a variety of reasons, some theological, some more deeply personal, I did become more committed to an Anglican tradition.

Later when I was Bishop of Tewkesbury and sharing in the life of different churches every Sunday, I counted it a privilege in the vast majority of churches to preside at a Eucharist alongside preaching a sermon, exercising in my view a genuinely Anglican emphasis on Word and Sacrament belonging together, complementing each other. Travelling round the diocese, visiting different churches every Sunday, I recognised that with the exception of a few Evangelical churches the vast majority of churches of all traditions were committed to holding together Word and Sacrament in a weekly Eucharist as the main Sunday service.

I have referred to the Parish Communion Movement in the 1950s. For some, this ran the risk of devaluing the preaching of the Word. The balance between Word and Sacrament tended to be weighted heavily in the direction of the Sacrament. With the emphasis on the Eucharist the normal expectation for the sermon slot was no more than 8–10 minutes. As bishop when visiting churches, I often made it clear that I was not prepared to be limited to 10 minutes! Donald Coggan during his ministry did a lot to have the importance of the sermon acknowledged. He was strongly committed to the importance of good biblical preaching. He wrote a helpful book on preaching: *The Sacrament of the Word* (later reprinted as *A New Day for Preaching*). The main argument of the book was that just as in the Eucharist bread and wine sacramentally become vehicles for receiving Christ so the words of a sermon can sacramentally be a vehicle for receiving Christ; there is something sacramental about the preaching ministry. The words of a sermon can be outward and visible signs of an inward and spiritual reality conveyed by the Holy Spirit.

Donald Coggan was very critical of modern church architecture which put a large Table/Altar central and only had a small lectern for preaching from. He felt this communicated a very unhelpful message about the place of the reading and preaching of Scripture over against the liturgy of the Eucharist. He said on more than one occasion that "sermonettes make Christianettes".

When I was Bishop of Tewkesbury, Cheltenham was in my patch. One of the Cheltenham churches where I preached on more than one occasion had been built in the Victorian era and had an enormous pulpit on wheels which in Victorian times would be wheeled out into the centre of the church dominating the church, a clear visual statement about the central importance of preaching. I have to say it was never rolled out for me and my preferred style of preaching was simply to stand at the chancel steps with an open Bible in my hand rather than go into a pulpit. On one occasion when preaching at a Mattins service in the presence of Prince Charles (now King Charles III), I was encouraged by the vicar to climb the pulpit steps up to the second stage pulpit in that church, not just six feet about criticism, but 12 feet above criticism!

As Bishop of Tewkesbury I shared in the training of Readers and gave lectures on preaching. As part of the course I got the students to reflect on the pros and cons of preaching from a pulpit. On the plus side there is an emphasis on the authority of the preaching ministry. However, as mentioned, my preferred style is simply to stand on a level with the members of the congregation. I believe that in our contemporary culture though there is a place for an authoritative declaration of God's truth that preaching is more about inviting congregation members into a conversation, encouraging them to view God's truth through the eyes of the preacher. Ideally the preacher has consulted commentaries, spent time reflecting on what a particular passage of the Bible's message is for this particular congregation at this particular time in its life and preaching that message prayerfully and dependent on the Holy Spirit to take the preacher's words and apply them in the hearts and minds and lives of the members of the congregation. I am also aware that whenever I preach to others before I do that I need to seek to apply God's Word to my own life and allow his Word through the ministry of the Holy Spirit to lead me into an ever deeper encounter with the living Christ, an ever deeper discipleship.

Is There Only One Way of Preaching Biblically?

As will be clear from the above I am deeply committed to the importance of biblical preaching. A related issue among many Evangelicals is what counts as biblical preaching. Is there only one right way of preaching? When I was on the staff of Wycliffe Hall, I was acting Principal for a short time after Geoffrey

Shaw retired and before Dick France was appointed as the new Principal. I was responsible for inviting preachers for the main mid-week service of Holy Communion and had invited Michael Bordeaux of Keston College. He preached in my view a deeply Christ-centred sermon drawing on the testimony of many Russian Christians at a time when the Church in Russia faced persecution. Later that evening I had a delegation of some of the "Reform" students visit me to say that if we had preachers like that again, they would be absenting themselves from the mid-week Communion service. Their complaint was that Michael Bordeaux had not taken a passage of the Bible and expounded it. In their view "Expository preaching" was the only proper form of preaching. I tried to help them see that his sermon was biblical throughout and Christ-centred and glorified Christ; I personally found his sermon deeply moving spiritually. However, I failed to convince them, sadly.

My own preferred approach to preaching is expository. I was privileged to serve my curacy at Emmanuel Church, Northwood, where my training incumbent David Bubbers adopted an expository approach to his sermons. I was also privileged when David Bubbers moved on to be General Secretary of the Church Pastoral Aid Society to have a year with Richard Bewes who was an extremely gifted expository preacher and later went on to be Vicar of All Souls, Langham Place, a key Church in the Conservative Evangelical tradition. In recognition of his preaching gifts, Richard was also a regular speaker at the Keswick Convention. While the focus of New Wine was Holy Spirit inspired worship alongside biblical teaching, the focus of the Keswick Convention since the nineteenth century has been on the faithful expository preaching of God's Word.

I will give some consideration in a later chapter to the place of preaching from the Lectionary in the Church of England. However, both David Bubbers and Richard Bewes chose to organise Sermon series at all services (apart from the 8.00 a.m. Prayer Book Communion service where we preached always on one of the passages chosen for that particular Sunday in the Prayer Book Lectionary), either a series on a particular book of the Bible or section of a book (I still recall a powerful series arranged by Richard Bewes on the Letters to the Seven Churches in the Book of Revelation and also a powerful series on the Book of Ecclesiastes) or a series of topics.

When I moved to be Vicar of Holy Trinity, Margate, because of my curacy experience I confess that I chose to organise Sermon series exclusively, though again at the 8.00 a.m. services of Holy Communion giving a short address on either the Epistle or Gospel chosen for that particular Sunday. Early on at Holy Trinity, I encouraged the PCC to embark on a significant building project. The Church already had two Church Halls but when I arrived, I found they were viewed simply as there to raise funds to enable the church to be financially viable. My first summer at the Church, I was keen to organise a Children's Holiday Club using Church Army personnel. It involved needing to have both Church Halls available. There was a problem because for the whole summer both Halls were let out to the local Language Schools bringing in a large amount of money. The PCC members were horrified that I was going to risk losing that significant income.

A Bible-based Approach to Giving

I digress briefly! Sorting out the Church's finances was quite a challenge. The Church had relied on fundraising events to balance the books. At Emmanuel, Northwood, I had been used to hearing sermons on biblical principles of giving and each year there was a major Gift Day preceded by a whole night of prayer and all the money raised was given away to projects in different parts of the world. I was aware that a whole night of prayer would be a step too far in Margate, but I was bold enough to suggest that we had a half-night of prayer and then a Gift Day on the Sunday. The Churchwardens to their credit went along with my in their view "mad idea". My predecessor had a Gift Day when he sat at the entrance to the Church on a Saturday and looked to people to come and make a gift. The amount raised on those Gift days had been about £200 for as long as the Churchwardens could remember and the money raised simply went into Church funds. I suggested that we set a target of £2400 and committed ourselves to giving it all away to projects linked with different Mission societies. Helpfully at the time, TEAR Fund had a project building houses in Bangladesh and it cost £45 to build a house and so several congregation members caught a vision of building one or more houses. I was more than a little nervous as we waited at the end of Evensong to hear whether our target of £2400 had been reached. Wonderfully, the amount raised was £2400 plus 25p! I never fully understood the 25p but a token perhaps that God more than provides for his people. For me it was an answer to prayer and several members of the congregation who had been drifting spiritually looked back later to that Gift Day weekend as a time when their faith revived and they became more committed disciples. Church finances came to be on a firmer footing and not reliant on fundraising events and we introduced having six Mission Societies that we supported (a two-month period for each and having someone from the Mission Society being supported to come on one of the Sundays to preach) as for too long the Church had focused solely on supporting itself and not supporting the Church in different parts of the world. End of digression!

Preaching Related to a Building Project over and against Preaching on the Lectionary

Because the two Church Halls were tied up with non-Church groups, I decided it would be helpful to have an additional building that could be solely available for Church activities and for mission outreach. So plans were drawn up for a Church

Lounge. Raising the funds was going to be quite challenging but at a PCC meeting, a clergy widow on the PCC suggested that we doubled the amount to be raised so we could give an equivalent amount to the Church in other parts of the world. Within about 5 minutes the PCC had voted in favour of her suggestion. So the challenge became even more demanding. However, wonderfully, the money all came in and Donald Coggan, at the time Archbishop of Canterbury and at that time also our diocesan bishop, came on a Sunday morning and dedicated the lounge for us, followed by a Church Fellowship meal in the newly opened Church Lounge. A congregation member took responsibility for organising a number of food based events in the lounge over the coming years as a very effective form of outreach to the wider community.

The point of this wider digression is related to preaching on the Lectionary and an important lesson I learnt as an Anglican Evangelical. Because I was encouraging the congregation to embark on a building project, I decided it would be good to run a sermon series on Haggai and Zechariah and Nehemiah who were all involved in building projects in Old Testament times. The idea was probably reasonable, but the timing wasn't good as it was Lent and a lot of congregation members complained that during Lent they felt the focus should be on the ministry of Jesus and preaching from the Lectionary on the gospel for the Sunday. The Baptist minister in Margate took no notice of liturgical seasons as that was not part of his spirituality; however, as an Anglican I should have been more in tune with Liturgical seasons which give a helpful rhythm to the Church's year with appropriate biblical passages for the different seasons. During my time as Vice-Principal of Wycliffe Hall (as a family we worshipped on Sundays at St Andrew's North Oxford, an Evangelical church) the focus once again was much more on sermon series rather than following the Lectionary. However, when I became an archdeacon and later as Bishop of Tewkesbury and I had an itinerant ministry with a few exceptions of some of the large Evangelical Churches, I found myself preaching Sunday by Sunday on one of the set Lectionary readings. The point has often been made that one of the advantages of preaching on the Lectionary is that it makes you preach on passages of Scripture that you might otherwise never preach on as over the course of a year the Bible is covered pretty fully in the set Lectionary readings. However, my experience has been that clergy who only preach on the Lectionary tend to focus almost exclusively on the gospel for the Sunday. I often deliberately chose as an archdeacon and as a bishop to preach on the Epistle and sometimes on the set Old Testament reading.

Word and Sacrament Together Increasingly Part of My Own Spiritual Life

Over a lifetime of ministry, the Eucharist has come to be increasingly important for nurturing my spiritual life alongside an important place for Scripture. When I retired in 2013 as Bishop of Tewkesbury, I chose to move to a House for Duty post in Chenies benefice on the edge of Oxford diocese with special responsibility for the church in Latimer. I inherited a monthly Prayer Book Mattins which was the least well attended service and so early on introduced a Prayer Book Communion service in its place so three out of the four Sundays each month were eucharistic. On the first Sunday which we retained as a non-eucharistic all-age service, I volunteered always to take the 8.00 a.m. 1662 Communion Service at Chenies and greatly valued being part of that very viable congregation once a month.

When in 2019 we moved to London in retirement and looked around for a church to make our spiritual home, we tried an Evangelical Anglican Church in Edgware which was reasonably close to where we lived, and we assumed we would enjoy being involved in the life of an Evangelical Church. However, two things made us unhappy to settle there. One factor was that the worship was exclusively full volume modern choruses and over the years though we value many of the Charismatic choruses and songs, we also greatly value the richness of many traditional Church of England hymns. The other factor was the main morning service was only a Eucharist once a month and increasingly our spiritual lives have been nurtured by sharing in a weekly Eucharist. So we explored other churches in the area and eventually settled on All Saints, Queensbury. The tradition is Liberal Catholic and many of our Evangelical friends are surprised we chose to settle there. However, a weekly Eucharist is important to us. The vicar preaches helpfully on Scripture and the worship is sensitively Spirit-filled in our view. An additional plus for us has been that it is a very mixed congregation with people from Sri Lanka, Pakistan, the West Indies, different African countries; a foretaste of the universal church gathered in heaven round the throne of the Lamb! Because of the Covid pandemic it hasn't been an easy three years though we continue to count it a privilege to be members of this congregation and the vicar is glad to make use of me!

On holiday in Belgium a few years back we visited Ghent Cathedral and I spent an hour gazing on the Adoration of the Mystic Lamb painted by Hubert and Jan Van Eyck in the fifteenth century with the Altar Piece installed in 1432. Inspired by passages in the Book of Revelation, this majestic work of art points to the centrality of the crucified Christ at heaven's worship and in my view could appropriately be interpreted in Eucharist terms. So sharing in the Eucharist regularly may well be a helpful preparation for spending eternity in worship of the triune God!

Word and Sacrament both equally important continue to nurture my spiritual life and I understand this partnership marks me out as an Evangelical in a specifically Anglican tradition over against a more Free Church Evangelical.

Chapter 4

Christian Belief Shaped through Prayer and Liturgy

I believe that a distinctively Anglican approach to theology and doctrine is to give an important place to liturgy in shaping our theology and our beliefs. Resolution 9 of the 1920 Lambeth Conference significantly referred to a rich diversity of devotion alongside a rich diversity of life.[6] There is a recognition that the words we share in saying together every time we gather as Christians for worship inevitably influence our beliefs.

Cranmer's 1662 Prayer Book and Liturgical Reform in the Twentieth Century

At the time of the Reformation Cranmer ensured that in the course of a year worshippers were exposed to an extremely rich diet of Scripture. The 1662 Lectionary envisaged worshippers being exposed to the whole of the Old Testament once and the whole of the New Testament twice over the course of a year and the psalms on a monthly basis. It was envisaged that lay people would join the clergy in daily worship and the daily engagement with Scripture. In addition, the 1662 Prayer Book is full of biblical allusions.

For 300 years the 1662 Prayer Book services were the only authorised services. I was brought up on the 1662 Prayer Book and its memorable poetic language undoubtedly has played an important part in shaping my own spirituality. However, during my lifetime there has been a considerable amount of liturgical revision. There were moves especially among more Anglo-Catholic clergy to allow greater freedom than the 1662 Prayer Book allowed. This resulted in a revised prayer book in 1927 approved by Church authorities. However, because the Church of England is the State Church the book needed the approval of Parliament and that failed to be given, largely through the influence of Evangelical Members of Parliament. A significant issue that was controversial was allowing the Reserved Sacrament. Though the 1928 Prayer Book was never officially authorised, many clergy made use of the alternatives provided within it over the following decades.

In 1965 Royal Assent was given to the *Prayer Book (alternative and other services) Measure* which essentially legalised the 1928 Prayer Book and especially the funeral service and the marriage service putting across a view of marriage more in keeping with contemporary views of marriage than the 1662 Prayer Book. No longer, for example, need a wife promise to obey her husband. My wife and I were married in 1968 and my wife's vicar insisted that we kept the traditional words of 1662 as he reckoned he knew my wife better than I did at that stage and I would never manage her unless she promised to obey! Our marriage, however, like most modern marriages, has been very much an equal partnership sharing decisions at every stage of our married life. Sadly during the time I have been working on writing this book, my wife, Rosemary, died having faced enormous health issues over a number of years. I have dedicated the book to her as over almost 55 years she has been my spiritual partner, my soul-friend and shared fully in my ministry; she has enriched my life and my ministry in countless ways over the years. She especially enriched my ministry as an archdeacon and as a bishop through her very special gift of hospitality.

The Series 3 services published between 1973 and 1980 consisted of a number of revised experimental services. The first was Holy Communion published in 1973. Infant Baptism was published in 1975. These various revisions were brought together in 1980 in the ASB (The Alternative Service Book) which was in use until 2000 when it was replaced with further significant revisions in Common Worship.

I will comment on what I see as two significant differences between the ASB and Common Worship. One difference is in the language. Because it was far from easy to find common ground between various theological views on the Liturgical Commission, many have commented on the *studied ambiguity* in much of the language of the ASB, allowing for different interpretations of the texts according to whether you had a more Catholic outlook or a more Evangelical outlook. The result was in my view that much of the language was very stilted. Common Worship offered 8 alternative eucharistic prayers (more have been made available since) allowing people of different theological persuasions to choose the eucharistic prayer(s) best suited to their outlook. The language of Common Worship in my view is much more poetical and potentially worshipful. One example that I have particularly come to value is the alternative post-communion prayer with its helpful allusions to the parable of the "prodigal son or better the two lost sons" in Luke 15 and powerful alliteration in the phrases "Dying and living he declared your love, gave us grace and opened the gate of glory". There is also helpful symmetry in the next three phrases in the prayer: "May we who share Christ's body live his risen life; we who drink his cup bring life to others; we whom the Spirit lights give light to the world."

Another difference was in the lectionary. The ASB Lectionary focused on themes for the different Sundays which encouraged preachers to preach on a theme common to the three readings and didn't in my view encourage a more expository approach to preaching. The Common Worship Lectionary moved away from thematic readings and the preacher is much more likely to focus on one of the readings (most clergy seem to opt each Sunday for the gospel reading which is a shame as there is great richness in the Old Testament readings and the Epistle passages are especially helpful for fostering deepening discipleship) rather than opt for a theme common to the three readings.

Changed Understanding of the Relationship between the Eucharist and the Cross

Looking over the entire period of liturgical innovation from the 1960s through to Common Worship there have been some significant changes in theological emphasis and if it is true as I believe it is that the words we say as Christians Sunday by Sunday play an important part in shaping our theological understanding, then these changes are potentially highly significant. I give as an example our understanding of the relationship between the Eucharist and the Cross and our understanding of the basis of our salvation. Cranmer's words captured in the 1662 Prayer Book Communion service are abundantly clear both in terms of his understanding of the relationship between the Eucharist and Christ's saving work on the cross but also his understanding of the basis of our salvation:

> Our Heavenly Father, who of thy tender mercy didst give thine only begotten Son Jesus Christ to suffer death upon the cross for our redemption, who made there by his one oblation of himself once offered, a full, perfect and sufficient sacrifice, oblation and satisfaction for the sins of the whole world.

There couldn't be a clearer statement of the Church of England Reformers' view of the cross as the place where our salvation is won and of substitutionary atonement. For some 300 years those words were heard by faithful Church of England worshippers on a weekly or at least a monthly basis, inevitably shaping their understanding of the place of the cross in the story of our salvation. On those occasions when I still have the privilege of presiding at a 1662 Communion service, my heart is warmed by Cranmer's words in the prayer of consecration. Those words encapsulate an Evangelical understanding of both the basis of our salvation and also of the Eucharist as cross-shaped.

While Evangelicals traditionally have majored on the cross as central to our faith, those of a more Anglo-Catholic persuasion have majored on the Incarnation. When we look at Common Worship Eucharistic Prayers (and before that the Alternative Service Book of 1980) the focus is no longer solely on the cross but a broader understanding of the basis of Christ's saving work which embraces the incarnation alongside the cross and also refers to Christ's resurrection and ascension. Eucharistic Prayer E alongside a reference to Christ's sacrifice made once for all upon the cross also includes these words: "We remember all that Jesus did." Prayer A specifically links the cross and incarnation and also includes the resurrection and ascension: "through him you have freed us from the slavery of sin, giving him to be born of a woman and to die upon the cross; you raised him from the dead and exalted him to your right hand on high." The focus of Common Worship Eucharistic Prayers is significantly different from the 1662 Prayer Book and as we share in listening to and repeating those words Sunday by Sunday, they cannot but influence our theological understanding.

The power of liturgy to shape our theology is also seen in the Ordinal. I have commented already on the fact that at the Reformation, the Church of England Reformers replaced the giving of a ciborium (for the wafers) and a chalice to the newly ordained with the giving of a Bible. This spoke volumes about a changed understanding of the focus of ordained ministry. In the contemporary Ordinal the ministry of the ordained priest is set very clearly in the context of the ministry of the whole people of God, an emphasis missing from the 1662 Ordinal. Moltmann, in his writings, has commented that the Reformers simply replaced a professional priest who operated alone at the altar with a professional priest that operated alone from a pulpit and it was to take more than another 300 years for the liberation of the whole people of God and taking on board the emphasis found in the New Testament (in 1 Corinthians 12,

Romans 12, Ephesians 4, 1 Peter 2 and 1 Peter 4) of ministry entrusted to the whole people of God. The twentieth century experienced a significant discovery of "every member ministry" especially through the Charismatic movement. Again, liturgy gives expression to changing understandings of Church and Priesthood and potentially plays a part in imbedding those changed views in the minds (and hearts) of contemporary worshippers.

Anglican Worship: Liturgical Rather Than Free

In relation to liturgy there is in my view another area where Anglican Evangelicals should give proper recognition to a distinctively Anglican approach to worship as liturgical as opposed to a more Free-Church tradition. As Bishop of Tewkesbury, on more than one occasion, I was delighted to attend a service in one of the leading Charismatic churches in the diocese of Gloucester. The form of worship had no recognisable Anglican elements in it even though on one occasion it was a Eucharist! The service consisted of a very large number of repeated worship songs, a short reading from the New Testament, a lengthy sermon and free eucharistic prayers prayed by the celebrant in his own words.

Liturgy Shaping Theology

A distinctively Anglican approach to worship is found in *Transforming Worship: Living a New Creation: A Report by the Liturgical Commission* (published in June 2007). The report has this significant statement: "The liturgy is essential to the formation of Christian community." We also read this in the Report: "The Church's worship is essential to the way in which the fundamental Christian narrative is transmitted from one generation to another."[7] An example of how specific phrases in the Eucharistic Prayers of Common Worship can shape our understanding of our faith and outworking of that faith in daily life is given from Eucharistic Prayer E: "Lord of all life, help us to work together for that day when your Kingdom comes and justice and mercy will be seen in all the earth." Also, a beautiful phrase from Eucharistic Prayer F is referred to: "Look with favour on your people and in your mercy hear the cry of our hearts. Bless the earth, heal the sick, let the oppressed go free and fill your Church with power from on high! **Amen. Come Holy Spirit.**" These liturgical prayers convey some very different emphases of living as Christians in the world from the more sharply individualistic spiritual approach of the 1662 Prayer Book Communion Service. In the light of historical lack of concern for the environment on the part of Christians the reference to blessing the earth is especially welcome and very appropriate in the twenty-first century aware as we are of global warming and our failure to care properly as good stewards for God's good creation.

The Report also argues "that at a profound level the Church's liturgy should sustain and express its unity". It argues in 2.15 that "throughout Christian history, the Church has shaped its worship by combining patterns of prayer, readings, silence and song to create a liturgical order, an order which can shape our own response and participation in the Christian story".[8] If we accept this Report as offering a distinctively Anglican understanding of worship, then the total freedom of worship in some Church of England Charismatic churches needs to be challenged to find a greater measure of distinctively Anglican worship. In passing we might wish to challenge the purely individualistic spirituality of many of the Charismatic worship songs. Also, we might wish to challenge those Church of England churches in an Anglo-Catholic tradition that use the Roman Missal about needing to come into line with distinctively Anglican eucharistic theology and worship.

Archbishop Stephen Cottrell when he was Bishop of Chelmsford, gave a lecture at St Paul's Cathedral on "A Good

Holy Week". He spoke of our Christian faith being a story before it is a statement. He spoke of the creed being deconstructed, laid out and populated and put back together again as a narrative for a life in which we are players on the stage and not just spectators in the stalls. He argued that when liturgies work well, we are converted afresh. Good liturgies draw us back to the central truths of our faith; the Holy Week liturgies remind us of our own death and of the implication of Christ's death for our lives. Holy Week liturgies encourage us to respond as we might to a great work of art or a participative drama.

The Place of Scripture in Anglican Liturgy

One significant characteristic shared by both the 1662 Prayer Book and Common Worship is the place of Scripture in Anglican worship shaping our Christian discipleship. This includes not only the specific reading of Scripture (the Lectionary implies an Old Testament and two New Testament readings at a Eucharist and in addition the use of a psalm though sadly very few churches include the reading of a psalm between the first two readings), but also a large number of Scriptural allusions and echoes in the prayers. Just one example is found in the second post-communion prayer: "When we were still far off you met us in your Son and brought us home", with a clear allusion to Jesus's Parable in Luke 15 of the Prodigal Son. I have already mentioned that the 1662 Lectionary envisaged worshippers being exposed to the whole of the Old Testament once and the whole of the New Testament twice over the course of a year and the psalms on a monthly basis. Scripture was seen and continues to be seen in Anglican practice as exercising a significant role in shaping Christian belief and practice. Again, I was concerned as a Bishop attending Charismatic churches that worship songs often far outstripped the place of the Bible; sometimes there was simply one very short Bible reading rather than the fuller coverage of Scripture envisaged in the Anglican Lectionary.

Chapter 5

Evangelicals and the Challenge of Hermeneutics

I have already referred to a significant gathering of Evangelicals at Keele University in 1967 and a fresh emphasis on the Eucharist at the heart of Sunday worship. There was also the beginning of a broader understanding of Mission and I shall be returning to that theme in a subsequent chapter. Ten years after Keele Anglican Evangelicals met again at Nottingham University on that occasion. I hadn't attended Keele but as Vicar of Holy Trinity, Margate, I attended the Nottingham Congress (NEAC). The full impact of that conference only came home to me as I spent time with students at Wycliffe Hall during my time there in the 1980s as Vice-Principal. A paper was delivered at NEAC by Tony Thiselton on hermeneutics and this paper had the potential to undermine many of the cherished convictions of Evangelicals. Indeed, as mentioned before many members of Reform (a Conservative Evangelical group in the Church of England) are convinced that the embracing of hermeneutics by many Evangelicals was a serious error that undermined what they saw as a Reformation principle of the plain sense of Scripture.

Biblical Hermeneutics acknowledges that how we read the Bible and interpret it will be influenced and indeed shaped by historical, social, political and personal contexts. To take one example, how a poor black woman in South Africa before the abolition of Apartheid might read parts of the Bible could be significantly different from the way a wealthy white businessman living in a leafy English suburb might understand and interpret the same texts. It was a recognition that our context can shape our reading of and interpretation of biblical texts.

Biblical Hermeneutics became a growth area during the latter half of the twentieth century. It featured especially in Liberation theology in Latin America and in South America among other parts of the world. The Exodus from Egypt was taken as a key text with a focus on liberation from all the forces that can enslave human beings. In 1994 I was privileged to spend a three-month Sabbatical at Tantur, a Roman Catholic Ecumenical Renewal centre situated between Jerusalem and Bethlehem. I undertook my own ecumenical study during my time at Tantur and wrote an article for the Roman Catholic Ecumenical Journal "One in Christ" exploring Koinonia (Fellowship) as a significant milestone on the road towards Church unity. As well as engaging in my own study I attended with my wife a number of the lectures that were on offer at Tantur. One especially rich series of lectures was given by Kenneth Bailey on the parables of Jesus in Luke's gospel. His interpretation of those parables was distinctive drawing on his experience of a lifetime spent in the Middle East and shaping his understanding of Jesus's parables. The fruit of a lifetime of living in a specifically Middle East cultural context has been written up by him in a number of books: *Poet and Peasant Through Peasant Eyes: Literary-cultural Approach to the Parables in Luke; Jesus through Middle Eastern eyes: Cultural Studies in the Gospels; Paul through Mediterranean Eyes: Cultural Studies in 1 Corinthians.* All these studies show how our being embedded in a particular culture can significantly shape our interpretation of the Bible. In seeking to interpret the teaching of Jesus to be embedded in the same cultural setting as he was, is particularly helpful.

Another series of lectures at Tantur that I attended was given by Naim Ateek. Naim is a Palestinian Arab but also an Israeli citizen. His family had to leave their home in 1948 when he was aged 11. His strong passion for justice shone through his lectures and is encapsulated in his book *Justice and Only Justice*. He adopts a Liberation theology approach but was aware that the normal Liberation Theological paradigm of the Exodus was far from helpful in the Israel-Palestine context and so he drew on the teaching of Jesus and especially the Sermon on the Mount to develop a theology appropriate to that unique context. Among other theological insights, he majors on the Old Testament emphasis that ultimately the Land belongs to God and we are only tenants.

I mention these two examples from my Sabbatical time in the Holy Land in 1994 and I shall be returning in a later chapter to the significance of Tantur in discovering the significance of "Holy Places", but for the moment I draw on my time there to illustrate the significance of cultural context in influencing our interpretation of Scripture.

Biblical Hermeneutics in the Latter Years of the Twentieth Century

Biblical Hermeneutics became a growth area during the latter half of the twentieth century. It featured especially in Liberation theology and in more recent times has resulted in a rich variety of theologies. Writers in Paula Gooder's book *Searching for Meaning: an Introduction to Interpreting the New Testament* identified at least eight different theological approaches to interpreting the New Testament in particular. Introducing these different approaches, Robert Fowler writes on Reader-Response Criticism. In its extreme form it leaves no room for arguing that one person's interpretation of the Bible has any greater degree of authority than anyone else's. The result is countless different interpretations of the same text, each equally valid.

As Bishop of Tewkesbury, I gave an occasional talk to ordinands and Readers on WEMTC (The West of England Ministerial Training Course) on Anglicanism. Referring to hermeneutics, I used an illustration from the world of music. One Saturday morning in the car I was listening to Radio 3 and I heard about eight different "interpretations" by different performers of Bach's Suites for solo cello. There were considerable differences in the interpretations. However, those playing couldn't just play any notes they felt like playing. Though there could be a rich variety of ways of interpreting the music, those varied interpretations were controlled by the notes written on the manuscript page and by any notes that Bach may have left about how he intended the pieces to be played. So there were limits to interpretation and it would be possible to argue that one interpretation was more authentic than another.

Applying this to the interpretation of the Bible, Tony Thiselton in his magnum opus on hermeneutics (Hermeneutics: An Introduction) has argued against any extreme form of subjectivism ("anyone's interpretation is as valid as anyone's else's") and a key factor is the so-called hermeneutical circle. Put simply, this means that our interpretation of the whole text is to be controlled by our interpretation of individual texts and in turn our understanding of individual texts is to be controlled by our understanding of the whole text (in this case the Bible as a whole). Thiselton has argued that such an approach safeguards us from slipping into total subjectivism and leaves open the possibility of arguing that one interpretation is more authentic than another. Recognising that the Bible is made up of 66 books written at different periods of history and offering a variety of theological approaches, we must, I believe, acknowledge that if we take hermeneutics seriously there will be no simplistic answers to what the Bible teaches. As already mentioned, the Reformers so-called *plain sense of Scripture* has to be carefully nuanced. Such a recognition should encourage us to be humble and gracious in responding to Christians who hold views different from our own and seeking to support their views from Scripture. In Anglican terms we would also acknowledge the place of Tradition down the centuries of Christian interpretation in influencing how we interpret the Bible and we would also draw on the *consensus fidelium*.

An Application to the Ordination of Women as Priests and Bishops

The recognition of hermeneutics in exploring the message of the Bible allowed many Anglican Evangelicals who had been opposed to the ordination of women as priests and bishops on the basis of certain "headship" texts to accept such ordinations, myself included. A helpful book in enabling many Evangelicals to accept biblical support for the ordination of women priests was Mary Hayter's doctoral thesis published as *The New Eve in Christ* in 1987 with its sub-title: "The Use and Abuse of the Bible in the Debate about Women in the Church."

At Wycliffe Hall, in my time, we had a number of Conservative Evangelical students who were strongly opposed to the ordination of women and some of them sadly failed to hold their strong views with humility and graciousness. We had quite a number of women ordinands visit Wycliffe with a view to possibly coming to train there and some of our male students would try to gang up on them at mealtimes and ask them why they were pursuing ordination when it was so clearly "contrary to Scripture". As staff we had to take steps to ensure that women ordinands visiting the college had sympathetic students sitting next to them at mealtimes to protect them from unhelpful challenges from some of these Conservative students.

Though by the time I was appointed to the staff of Wycliffe Hall, I was already strongly in favour of the ordination of women, the calibre of the women who came to train and the genuineness of their sense of call by God and the quality of their gifts confirmed me even more strongly in being convinced that it was God's will for his Church.

The Anglican principle of the *consensus fidelium* (agreement among Christians at any given time and over time) has also played a part. As in the early Church as recorded in Acts 15 when there was strong disagreement among the first Christians on an issue, the Church leaders were able to write "it seemed good to the Holy Spirit and to us" so there has been a sense of "the mind of the Church" guided by the Holy Spirit on this still potentially sensitive issue. A substantial majority in both the Church of England and the wider Anglican Communion has come to embrace enthusiastically the ordination of women both as priests and as bishops, however, a significant minority remain unconvinced that this development is consistent with biblical teaching.

There is a further factor to be taken into consideration and that is that the Church of England (and the wider Anglican Communion) is not the sum total of the Christian Church, and Roman Catholics and Orthodox Christians have not accepted the position adopted by the Church of England and, indeed, the decision by the Church of England led to more strained ecumenical relationships especially with the Orthodox Communion. Because we are part of a divided and fractured world-wide church, it is less straightforward to speak of a *consensus fidelium*.

In a fractured world-wide Church decisions taken by one denomination ideally need to acknowledge that such decisions may make the path to Church Unity more challenging and complex.

Reflections on the Nature of Christian Unity

I have referred in passing to the privilege of spending three months at Tantur in Jerusalem (the Roman Catholic Ecumenical Renewal Centre) for a Sabbatical in 1994 while Archdeacon of Surrey. I had planned to spend my Sabbatical in Oxford in the Bodleian library (not the most exciting way to spend a Sabbatical!), but the Revd Frank Telfer in charge of clergy development in Guildford diocese encouraged me to consider spending the time at Tantur. At the time I hadn't heard of Tantur, so I did some research into it and liked what I learned about it. It was established by the Pope after the Second Vatican Council as a centre for ecumenical study and spiritual renewal. It is largely funded through the generosity of the Roman Catholic University of Notre Dame in the States. There is also a British Trust for Tantur which historically has helped to fund clergy and ordinands to share in courses at Tantur. I later became a member of the Trust and for several years chaired it. Tantur runs month-long and three-month long courses. Frank Telfer wanted me to spend at least part of my Sabbatical at Tantur on my own. I told him that because my wife, Rosemary, had always been fully involved in my ministry and because with a very busy ministry we didn't always spend as much time together as we would like, I wanted her to be with me for the whole three months. It was a bit of a battle, but I won in the end! Rosemary signed up for the three-month course and I signed up for engaging in my own study but with the freedom to attend any of the lectures on offer on the three-month course, and to share in the various educational trips. I have already referred to the lectures given by Kenneth Bailey on the Parables of Jesus in Luke's gospel and these lectures given three times a week were a real highlight for me, inspirational and fascinating in highlighting Middle Eastern perspectives on the parables of Jesus drawing on Kenneth Bailey's life-long experience of living in the Middle East.

Dame Mary Tanner lived in Guildford diocese and so I arranged a session with her to pick her brains before heading off to Tantur. Mary had an academic background teaching Old Testament but also had an incredibly broad experience of ecumenical work. She was European President of the World Council of Churches (WCC) from 2006–2013. From 1974 she was a member of the Faith and Order Commission of WCC and was its Moderator from 1991–1998. She helpfully suggested a number of books and also articles in ecumenical journals to read. Tantur as an Ecumenical centre and with a well-stocked library, was an ideal place to undertake my study. Mary was also able to put me in touch with the editor of the Roman Catholic Ecumenical Journal *One in Christ* and so my study was directed towards writing an appropriate article for that journal. In consultation with Mary, I decided to explore the extent to which Koinonia represented a significant milestone on the road to Christian unity.

In my article I referred to Mary's own article in *Ecumenical Review* written in preparation for the Fifth World Conference on Faith and Order (January 1993) in which she identified Koinonia as "the most promising theme of contemporary ecumenical theology" and "offering a portraiture of the unity of the Church" drawing together different strands.

In my article I explored whether Koinonia was a helpful New Testament model for unity. Schuyler Brown in a 1976 article in *One in Christ* argued against George Vandervelde who claimed that Koinonia tells us nothing about Paul's ecclesiology though Brown was cautious about claiming too much for Koinonia. In my view, Koinonia (literarily the word refers to ideas or experiences held in common) is a helpful overarching word that holds together both unity and diversity in the New Testament's understanding of the nature of the Church. I argued on the basis of 1 John 1, 3–7 that Koinonia helpfully draws together both a vertical relationship with a Trinitarian God enjoyed by all Christians and at the same time a horizontal relationship with other Christians. Within our own Anglican theological tradition of "comprehensiveness", there is similarly a helpful focus on unity in diversity, an acknowledgment of the different traditions that historically have contributed to our distinctive Anglican understanding of the Church.

Ecumenical Experience at Tantur in Jerusalem, Enriching My Christian Understanding

One of the statements we affirm as Christians in the Nicene Creed is that we believe that the **Church is one**. Some Christians look back to a golden age of the Church in New Testament times when they believe that the Church was totally united. Certainly, Luke in his portrayal of the early Church seeks to convey an idealistic picture of the unity of the Church. However, reading between the lines we find that there were tensions between Christians from a Jewish background and those from a Gentile background. Barnabas and Paul had a very sharp disagreement over whether it was appropriate to include John Mark in their ongoing missionary journeys and they went their separate ways. Paul in his Corinthian letters is clear that there were divisions between different groupings among the Christians in Corinth and the fact that Paul often (e.g., Philippians 2, 1–3) urges a spirit of unity between Christians with whom he corresponds suggests that there was in the background always a threat of division. Jesus prayed (John 17) that his followers might be one, but down the history of the Church sadly divisions have always been more characteristic of the life of the Church than unity.

Early on there were theological divisions over the nature of the Trinity and over the Person of Christ. It is over-simplistic to argue that the "orthodox" were those whose views were based on Scripture as both sides in these discussions backed up their claims by quoting biblical texts. In 1054 there was the Great Schism between the Eastern and Western Churches. Then at the Reformation the Church in the West fragmented even more with different understandings of the Eucharist, of Baptism, of the nature of the Priesthood and even the nature of the Church itself. Tragically, Christians killed one another over these strongly held divisive opinions. The twentieth century saw the rise of the Ecumenical Movement and numerous theological discussions between divided denominations. Those who shared in these discussions often found themselves moving towards a strong sense of mutual understanding and acceptance, but such forward progress was then often undermined by the different Churches' official responses to the ecumenical reports.

Within the different theological traditions there have been different understandings of the nature of unity. The Roman Catholics and Orthodox have majored on organic union, one physically united Church. They have taken the view that before there can be eucharistic hospitality there has to be doctrinal agreement on the nature of the Eucharist and the nature of priestly ministry. Evangelicals in contrast and those of a Pentecostal persuasion have majored on a spiritual communion that transcends our organic divisions. The Keswick Convention (where Christians from different denominations come together for worship and biblical teaching in the summer in the Lake District) has had this slogan *All one in Christ*. In contrast to that Evangelical tradition Christians of a rich variety of backgrounds have discovered a spiritual unity at Taize with its simple repetitive worship songs.

At Tantur each group of participants in a three-month course were allowed to make their own decision about eucharistic hospitality. Our group decided to have an open table policy. Though Thomas Stransky, the rector of the time, personally didn't approve of an open eucharistic table he was content to allow us to make that decision. The majority of those participating in the three-month course were Roman Catholic priests (mostly from the States). When one of them was presiding at the daily midday Eucharist, Rosemary and I were welcome to receive the sacrament. When I was presiding, the majority of the Roman Catholic priests honoured me by receiving the bread and wine from me. One priest who didn't was Father Giles Pater. A few years later I was invited to give two lectures in the States on the Decade of Evangelism and during our time in Washington, I had the privilege of being invited to preside and preach at a midday Saturday Eucharist in Washington Anglican Cathedral. Father Giles had travelled some distance to join us for the service. Shortly before the moment of distribution he left the service and I assumed that sadly he still felt unable to receive the sacrament from me; for him it was a question of obedience to his Church authorities. However, he had left to answer a call of nature and he returned shortly afterwards and came forward to receive the bread and wine from me. I confess that there were tears in my eyes at that point; a very special moment of sensing our oneness in Christ.

In my article for *One in Christ* I argued on the basis of my experience at Tantur that rather than viewing sharing in eucharistic fellowship as the climax of discovering doctrinal unity, to share together at the same table led to a deeper spiritual oneness which potentially was able to transcend doctrinal differences. It is not to pretend that doctrinal differences are of no importance but to recognise that in spite of such differences it is possible to discover an ever deeper spiritual unity through sharing in a common table. I also argued that the value of focusing on Koinonia in ecumenical relationships is that it allows for a unity that can embrace a great deal of diversity; unity in diversity modelled on a Trinitarian theology.

Sharing a common life with Christians of very different spiritual traditions over three months I found opened me up to acknowledge valuable insights into spiritual practices that were totally foreign to my Evangelical tradition. In my article I referred to one of the Notre Dame students (a group of ten students from the Roman Catholic Notre Dame University in the States spent a semester at Tantur during our time there in the Spring of 1994) whom my wife and I got to know well who made a daily practice of spending time reverencing the Host in a chapel set aside for such devotion. Having listened to her reflect on how this deepened her love for Jesus, I felt I should step inside the chapel one morning and I had an overwhelming sense of the presence of the risen Christ in that tiny chapel. I have not added adoration of the blessed sacrament to my spiritual practices, and I continue to remain suspicious of the theology underlying the practice of the adoration of the reserved sacrament, but it led me to acknowledge the genuineness of this spiritual practice for other Christians rather than write it off as an unsound practice which in my earlier days I would have been tempted to do.

A particularly close friendship developed between Rosemary and myself and a Redemptorist priest, James Wallace. We later had the privilege of spending time with him in Washington and he spent time with us when I was Bishop of Tewkesbury. He was well known in Roman Catholic circles as a lecturer in homiletics (the study of preaching) and on one of his visits to spend time with us, I was able to get him to lead a day for clergy in the diocese of Gloucester on preaching. There would be several theological areas where he and I would not see eye to eye but through our friendship and spending time together at Tantur we subsequently came to value a deep sense of oneness in Christ, a oneness that transcended our theological differences. During the Covid lockdown we were privileged through Zoom to join him in the Mass celebrating the fiftieth anniversary of his ordination as a priest, a Mass shared with his fellow Redemptorist priests in Washington and including concelebration. I have never been very keen on the practice of concelebration as in my view the whole congregation together with the priest are the celebrants at the Eucharist, but I have to admit that this special Mass was a deeply spiritual experience for my wife and myself. In part I guess it was because of our deep friendship with James, but I believe it was more than that, reflecting the presence of the risen Christ in those Redemptorist priests and in the special celebratory Mass.

I have mentioned that as a result of my Sabbatical at Tantur, I became a Trustee of the British Trust for Tantur. Peter Coleman, retired Bishop of Crediton, was chairman at the time. George Carey had been chairman for a while before becoming Archbishop of Canterbury and retained a great interest in the work of the Trust. He facilitated funding for a significant ecumenical pilgrimage under the title of Journey of Reconciliation. When later I was

Chair, we funded a second Ecumenical Pilgrimage again called a Journey of Reconciliation. The participants were drawn from a very wide cross-section of denominations, including Baptists, Methodists, Roman Catholics, Anglicans, Orthodox, Black Pentecostal, Salvation Army, The Society of Friends. Living together and sharing in worship together (especially eucharistic worship) was extremely challenging, but all who shared in the Pilgrimage testified to it being a life-transforming experience that challenged deeply held Christian convictions. In 2020 I handed over the Chair to Professor Judith Lieu whom my wife and I had come to know well at Tantur in 1994 when she was a visiting scholar. The British Trust are looking to organise a third Journey of Reconciliation in 2024, this time for Christians under the age of 35. Tragically, as I write events in the Middle East led to this Pilgrimage needing to be postponed.

My time in Tantur also significantly influenced my understanding of the complex relationships between Israelis and Palestinians in Israel/Palestine. After our time at Tantur Rosemary and I started leading pilgrimages to the Holy Land. One pilgrimage proved very challenging as most of the group (ourselves included) felt considerable sympathy for the plight of Palestinians but one member of the group was a very strong Zionist and expressed his views very forcibly. It was challenging as a leader to maintain unity within the group and a willingness to listen respectively to each other.

Reflecting on Koinonia as a helpful theological model for unity in diversity, I have come to believe that Koinonia could potentially be a helpful way for Anglicans at a time when we threaten to be pulled apart and fragmented through strongly held conflicting theological and ethical views within the wider Anglican Communion as well as within the Church of England, and I shall return to these reflections in a later chapter on the history of the Lambeth Conferences and especially recent history.

Chapter 6
Evangelicals and a Commitment to Evangelism

In Chapter 5 I talked about the impact of hermeneutics and Ecumenical Relationships in general on the Evangelical world and especially on my own spiritual journey. Another significant theological area where many Evangelicals, myself included, found themselves reassessing their understanding was that of **Mission**.

I have already made reference to the gathering of Anglican Evangelicals at Keele University in 1967 with reference to many Anglican Evangelicals recognising the importance of putting the Eucharist at the heart of the local Church's Sunday worship. One reflection on the significance of the Keele Congress at the time expressed it this way: "a widely acknowledged major watershed for the Evangelical Movement in the Church of England – there was a decisive attitudinal shift at the congress, driven especially by the younger generation – from piety to policy, from conservatism to radicalism, from homogeneity to diversity and from exclusivism to ecumenism" (Andrew Atherton in the *Journal of Anglican Studies*).

My main focus in this book is on Anglican Evangelicals but there was during this time a wider movement among Evangelicals of all denominations through the Lausanne Movement. The first International Congress on World Evangelisation was held at Lausanne in 1974. A highly significant individual at the Lausanne Congresses was John Stott, Rector of All Souls, Langham Place, and a leading Anglican Evangelical in the twentieth century.

Before the 1970s, Evangelicals had majored on personal salvation as the heart of the gospel and most were very wary of a focus on working to bring about social and political change in spite of the great tradition of earlier Evangelicals working for change: slavery, children working in the mines and other social and political issues. I remember from my curacy days my vicar, David Bubbers, using an illustration that majored on the central importance of personal salvation: a young boy was given a jigsaw for his birthday of all the countries of the world. Because his geographical knowledge was not great, he struggled to complete the jigsaw. However, this jigsaw was unusual. On the other side of the pieces was a picture of a human being. Because the boy was very familiar with what a human being looked like, by turning the pieces of the jigsaw over he was able to complete the jigsaw easily. He then turned the jigsaw pieces back over and lo and behold there was a picture of the different countries of the world. The message was clear: get the individual right and the world will fall into place. Though in the past I have been happy to use this illustration myself, I came to believe that it conveyed an over simplistic approach to complex social and political issues in every part of the world and at every stage of human history. In my next chapter I shall focus on a broadening understanding of Mission, but in this chapter I plan to focus on Evangelism as a characteristic commitment on the part of Evangelicals and changing approaches to and understanding of the nature of evangelism.

I trained for ordination at Oak Hill Theological College. At the time Maurice Wood who had previously been Vicar of St Mary's, Islington, and later went on to be Bishop of Norwich was Principal of Oak Hill; at heart he was an Evangelist and saw evangelism as being at the heart of ministry as an ordained person. When he was vicar in Islington, he produced a series of "Islington Booklets" explaining the gospel in simple terms to help someone become a Christian and then a number of booklets to foster growth in the Christian faith. When later he was Bishop of Norwich, the booklets were given a new title of "Norwich

Booklets"! David Bubbers, the vicar I served my curacy with, again saw evangelism as being at the heart of parish ministry.

To be an Evangelical is to be committed to the "evangel", the gospel and sharing the gospel. The phrase "born again" is often used by Evangelicals to emphasise a living faith as opposed to a nominal faith. The terminology is found in John 3 where the evangelist records a late-night meeting Jesus has with a religious leader called Nicodemus. Jesus tells this religious leader that he needs to "be born again" (the Greek word could also suggest "be born from above" – a heavenly new birth), to be born both of water and the Spirit; natural human birth and a spiritual new birth. The imagery of new birth is found in many other parts of the New Testament, in the letters of Paul, in 1 Peter, in the letter to the Hebrews. As mentioned earlier, I had a spiritual experience at 18 through reading the account of St Paul's conversion in Acts 9 which I later identified as being "born again".

During my curacy, we had a year of outreach under the title "God First". Congregation members were encouraged to invite friends and neighbours to a series of special services many with a guest preacher and an invitation (Billy Graham style) for people to come forward after the sermon to make a personal commitment. There were a number of people, mostly a husband or wife where the other partner was already a committed Christian, who responded positively during this special year of mission, but it didn't result in greatly increased numbers of new Christians. The week-in, week-out ministry was such that in the course of a year, a number of new people would discover a living faith in Christ and get involved more fully in the life of the Church.

As an Anglican Evangelical I believed that the parish was important, and I had a spiritual responsibility to ensure that as many parishioners as possible had an opportunity to hear the good news of Jesus and be encouraged to make a response. The

Occasional Offices of baptisms, marriages and funerals were seen as providing unique opportunities for sharing the gospel with those requesting to have their babies baptised (I will return to this later), getting married in church and requesting the funeral of a loved one either in church or at a local Crematorium. During my time on the staff at Wycliffe Hall, I had to challenge some of our Reform students that there was a distinctive approach to being an Evangelical in the Church of England. They were tempted to argue that when they got to a parish they would fill their diaries with one-to-one appointments to share the gospel and would then claim that they were too busy to fit in requests for a baptism or a wedding or a funeral of a non-church person. For me this was a Free-Church Evangelical approach rather than a distinctively Anglican Evangelical approach where we have a responsibility to all parishioners whether or not they attend church.

In the 1960s the Revd Dick Rees led what he called Prayer Book Missions. These were evangelistic with a distinctively Church of England ethos. He encouraged a church that had signed up for one of his missions to go through their registers to identify all those who had had babies baptised, been married in church or had the funeral of a loved one and invitations would be sent out to all these people to come and share in a special service (for example, wedding couples to renew their marriage vows) where Dick Rees would give a clear gospel message and invite a response.

Evangelism among Young People

In the 1960s and 1970s Evangelical Churches invested a great deal of time and energy in reaching out to young people. It was customary for the new curate to be given responsibility for an area of youth work. When I arrived at Emmanuel, Northwood, there was already a curate, Tim Watson, who had responsibility for a youth group known as Guild for young people aged 16–18. I was asked to get involved with a youth group called Saturday Club for 14–16 year olds. In addition, there were boy Covenanters and girl Covenanters. The boy covenanter group was particularly flourishing led by Herbert Hackett who worked for Covenanters nationally. Many congregation members at Emmanuel, Northwood, were professional people and quite wealthy. However, all around the church were Council Houses and Herbert Hackett was especially successful in reaching out to boys from that Estate.

When I was first involved with Saturday Club (which at the time was lay led, my predecessor as curate, who was an older man, had not been involved with youth ministry; he left Church of England ministry on the issue of infant baptism among other issues where he was increasingly unhappy with the Church of England) numbers had tailed off and many parents with kids in that age group had lost confidence in the leadership for various reasons. I set about systematically visiting the young people in their homes and over a period of time, numbers began to grow as confidence in the group was renewed. We used to meet three times a week: Saturday evenings for a social evening, ice skating, ten pin bowling, car treasure hunts, tramp suppers and similar events; on a Sunday evening after church the young people crowded into our curate's house for a time of worship and a talk; on Wednesday evenings we met in the home of one of the young people for Bible study – we eventually had up to 30 young people joining in with the Wednesday Bible studies. At that time there weren't the same pressures of homework on youngsters as there would be now.

Over the New Year we took away 100 or so young people for a "Houseparty" involving fun activities, discussion groups, worship and talks. In August we took 36 young people away each year on a Continental Holiday in six vans, each with a driver, a "mum" (older girl as a leader) and 6 young people. In my time we visited Austria, Bled in what was Yugoslavia, Sweden and

Bavaria. Many young people found these times away over the New Year and in the summer very helpful times for growing in their Christian faith. Inevitably, quite a number of these young people didn't keep up with their Christian faith in adult years. However, as I have moved around the country in ministry, I have often come across former Saturday Club members strongly involved in the life of their local church; a number went on to be ordained, (one ended up as a bishop!), several ended up in various parts of the world engaged in missionary work and large numbers were involved in leadership in their local churches. Recently, sadly my wife died and we had her funeral service at Emmanuel, Northwood, before burial in the Churchyard in Latimer where I had served as House for Duty priest. It was very heart-warming that quite a number of the young people from our curacy days turned up at Rosemary's funeral. Shortly after the funeral one of the former Saturday Club members (she is now 70!) and her husband contacted me and invited me over to lunch; they still live in Northwood and are very involved in the life of Emmanuel. She came from a non-Christian home at the invitation of friends at school and had to battle with her dad who wasn't at all happy with her attending church! After lunch before I headed home, she asked whether she could pray for me; I was delighted to accept. I believe that getting involved in ministry and evangelism among young people represented taking full advantage of the opportunities afforded by being the State Church, with an open door into homes. However, in those days my main focus was on the spiritual life of individual Christians and looking back, I failed at that time to grasp the social and political implications of the gospel.

Evangelism Explosion: Lessons Learned from an American Presbyterian Church

Evangelicals also believe every Christian has a responsibility to share the gospel with others, not a task simply left to the clergy. However, lay Christians are often reluctant evangelists, often not wishing to embarrass friends or family or not having confidence to be able to deal with objections that may be raised against the Christian faith. In terms of putting evangelism firmly on the agenda of the local church during my curacy and offering a very practical way for lay Christians to grow in confidence in sharing their faith, I was introduced to Evangelism Explosion.

A member of the congregation was a close friend of members of the Billy Graham Association. He ran an engineering business in the early 1970s which took off and overnight he became a millionaire. Through his American links he was aware of a church in America, Coral Ridge Presbyterian Church in Fort Lauderdale in Florida, which had grown from a tiny congregation to a congregation of over 8000 through a basic lay training programme that set out to equip lay people to be confident in sharing their faith. The programme title of "Evangelism Explosion" was not the most helpful title and its British expression later became "Teach and Reach". The Church ran "Clinics" regularly drawing people from around the world to catch the vision of lay training in faith sharing and to be trained in the Evangelism Explosion approach.

The member of the congregation decided this programme could be helpfully applied in Northwood. He paid for our vicar, David Bubbers and his wife, Evelyn, to go out for one of their ten-day Clinics. David's response on his return was positive and in November 1973 my wife, Rosemary, and I were asked whether we too would like to attend a Clinic at Coral Ridge Presbyterian Church. It was too attractive an offer to turn down especially as the church member who funded the trip wanted us to visit three other places in the States after the conference. We were privileged to have a day in Washington, a day in New York and a day at Niagara Falls. It was a truly memorable two weeks. My mother kindly came and looked after our two young sons so my wife, Rosemary, was able to attend the "clinic" with me.

The programme was very regimented. People went out in teams of three. One was the trained leader; the other two were learning on the job. You were encouraged to learn particular Bible verses off by heart and to present the gospel in a very routine way. After initial pleasantries, conversation was opened up with two key questions: "If you were to die tonight would you be sure of going to heaven?" Then a follow up question: "Suppose you were to die tonight and stand before God and he asked you, why should I let you into my heaven, what would you say?" The focus was two-fold: on Christian assurance and grace rather than good works as the basis for our salvation. This then led to a five-point summary of the gospel, starting with the problem of human beings as sinners, judgement and Christ's death on the cross as the answer and the resurrection with an invitation to invite the risen Christ into one's life. Surprisingly, there was no reference to the work of the Holy Spirit. The programme had emerged under Jim Kennedy, the Presbyterian Pastor, in a cultural context where large numbers of Americans had some kind of Church involvement and Christian understanding but may not have grasped the centrality of grace in their engagement with the Christian story. So the particular approach was well suited to securing a positive response in many of those visited or engaged with in Street Evangelism. I had the privilege of sharing the gospel with a retired couple visiting Fort Lauderdale during one of our times engaging in Street Evangelism and inviting them to pray a prayer of commitment with me, there was no sense of embarrassment or awkwardness in the conversation with them.

One area which I was not totally comfortable with was the tendency to treat every objection that was raised as a red herring rather than a genuine issue to be addressed and so to encourage the participants to have stock answers to most of the standard questions that people tend to raise. Part of the training included a reflection on Jesus's conversation with the Samaritan woman recorded in John 4 where when the woman seeks to divert the conversation which had become rather uncomfortable to a safe discussion about where worship should take place. Jesus doesn't let her off the hook but brings her firmly back to having to face up to the key question of his identity. I would want a more nuanced response to questions especially those relating to the problem of human suffering. As I write this earthquakes in Turkey and Syria have resulted in loss of life and suffering on a massive scale and flooding in Libya has resulted in massive loss of life. Slick answers in such situations are very inappropriate and don't carry much weight.

One thing about the Church that disturbed us but was typical of America in the early 1970s was their attitude to Black people. The Church was entirely white and there was a kind of apartheid in the churches in Fort Lauderdale with totally separate churches for white Christians and for Black Christians. That at the time seemed to me to undermine a key gospel principle of Christ breaking down the barriers that so often divide human beings one from another to create a new united humanity. We were guests and only there for a very short period of time so I didn't feel it was appropriate to challenge them over this, but it left a very uncomfortable feeling in us that the message of reconciliation at the heart of the gospel as explored especially in the fifth chapter of St Paul's second letter to the Corinthians was not being lived out in the life of the Christian community.

Once back in Northwood, David Bubbers was keen to introduce Evangelism Explosion to the parish. A number of lay people were approached and invited to join in an initial training programme and then to go out in teams of three to visit various homes. A list was drawn up of those who had some kind of link with the church, through the baptism of a child, through having children or young people in the different church organisations, through having visited the church and filled in a visitor's card. A letter was then sent out explaining that a team of three church members would like to pay them a visit on a particular evening to talk about the Christian faith. A surprising number of people welcomed the visitors (it was the kind of area where it was felt that it was the polite thing to do and would be rather rude to refuse a visit). This cultural setting sometimes made it difficult to be sure how people were actually responding during the evening and there was certainly a risk of people politely listening to what the visitors had to say and agreeing to pray with them at the end of the evening rather than disagree with them. However, there were undoubtedly several individuals who came to a living faith through Evangelism Explosion during my time as curate and I am aware of some of them forty-plus years on still active Christians; the son of one woman who became a Christian at the time went on to be ordained.

A fringe benefit for those who shared in Evangelism Explosion, going out once a week to knock on doors and spend time in people's homes, was that their own faith was greatly strengthened and their confidence in sharing their Christian faith. A couple whom we involved in the training (at the time he was a Security Officer in the RAF) found their faith greatly deepened and the husband went off to train for ordained ministry, taking the costly decision to pull out of the RAF to train a year earlier than would have secured him a much more sizeable pension. He and his wife subsequently exercised a fruitful and costly ministry in a tough area of Birmingham and later among the Inuit in Northern Canada, their faith renewed and deepened through involvement in Evangelism Explosion, resulting in a lifetime of dedicated costly service and ministry.

I went on from the curacy in Northwood to be Vicar of Holy Trinity, Margate. Because I had a generally positive experience of Evangelism Explosion, I decided to make use of it early on for baptism visits. One woman came to faith through my wife sharing the gospel with her in an Evangelism Explosion way, but that was the only positive outcome. However, we found people growing over a period of time into Christian faith through attending our informal Morning Services. There was a Church of England Secondary School in addition to two single sex Grammar Schools in the area. To get your child into the Church of England Secondary School you had to get the signature of your local vicar to confirm that you attended their church. I was always aware when the time was approaching for applying for entrance to the school as new parents would appear on a Sunday morning. Some stopped attending once their child was admitted to the school, but the vast majority continued to attend; many of them joined an adult confirmation group which I led in the vicarage and over a period of time, grew into discipleship.

Many Evangelicals in the 1960s expected "genuine" Christians to be able to name the day and even the hour when they "invited Christ to come into their lives". The Billy Graham Crusades took place in the 1950s and later fostered such an understanding of conversion. However, during the 1980s and later many Anglican Evangelicals came to recognise that there are many different ways in which people become Christians, and for many it is a slow growth into discipleship over many months or even years rather than a single moment in time. My experience of people coming to faith at Holy Trinity, Margate, was that for the majority they grew into discipleship through attending Sunday morning worship on a regular basis and having a growing and deepening sense of encountering the risen Christ through worship and Christian fellowship.

However, as an Evangelical I also believed it was important to create opportunities for people on a spiritual journey to make a commitment. Initially, the curate and I organised special weekends four times a year (later we realised that was too frequent and reduced to twice a year) when I would invite an evangelist (on two occasions we had Keith de Berry who brought a team of young people from his retirement base in

London; we also had Vijay Menon, a converted Hindu and also I invited my former vicar, Richard Bewes). The format was very traditional encouraging Church members to lay on a coffee morning or afternoon tea or a supper party and invite friends and neighbours along; a team member would share their personal faith and open up discussion and then the team leader would preach an evangelistic sermon at the Sunday services. On one weekend in June, we laid on a barbecue in the spacious vicarage garden, and on that occasion Keith de Berry preached an evangelistic message standing on the small balcony outside our upstairs bedroom! Some 400 people attended the barbecue; it was evidence of the value of friendships and links that can easily be nurtured through the networks provided by a Church of England parish church.

Another area of development in my own thinking about conversion and coming to faith is related to over simplistic presentations of the gospel and a belief that the gospel can be encapsulated in a simple formula. Though I valued my involvement with Evangelism Explosion and believe there is a place for clarity in sharing the essential beliefs that Christians hold, I would now wish to place more emphasis on the key component being a personal encounter with Christ. Within the Anglican tradition those of a more Catholic persuasion have majored on the Incarnation; those of a more Evangelical persuasion have majored on the cross. I believe within the Anglican tradition there is a reluctance to focus on one way of presenting the gospel. My unhappiness with the over standardised and simplistic presentation of Evangelism Explosion would apply as well to the Four Spiritual Laws of Campus Crusade, Journey into Life by the late Archdeacon Norman Warren. I would have similar reservations about Alpha while acknowledging the enormous number of people who have been helped to a living faith through Alpha. It represents a fuller more systematic presentation of Christian truth and has a helpful emphasis on the work of the Holy Spirit, something that I noted with surprise was missing in Evangelism Explosion. Experiencing Alpha in a variety of churches over a number of years, I came to believe that a significant factor in its effectiveness was the meal and the place of fellowship and the freedom to ask questions in the small groups. In Anglican terms it is, I believe, a mistake that no reference is made to the sacraments. When I was approached as Archdeacon of Surrey to lead an Alpha course for St Andrew's, Farnham, a church at that time in the Liberal Catholic tradition, I added two extra sessions to Alpha on the sacraments, believing that was important for a church in the Anglican tradition.

After special times of outreach, my curate, the Revd Prebendary David Perryman (he led the youth work when I was curate and later went on to be ordained), was particularly helpful in recognising the importance of putting structures in place that enabled those who had made a response to grow in their new-found faith. He had a very helpful analytical approach and noted that "new" Christians flourished most where two factors combined: involvement in a small group together with one-to-one ongoing support. He also had a healthy emphasis on the part played by the Holy Spirit in fostering spiritual growth.

The Gospel as Cross-Shaped

An issue related to evangelism for many Evangelicals historically is what the heart of the gospel is. The gospel is seen as cross-shaped. St Paul writing to the Christian Church in Corinth stated that he had made a decision not to know anything among them except Jesus Christ and him crucified. A key doctrine for many Evangelicals is substitutionary atonement. They depend on Mark 10, 45 among other key verses where Jesus is recorded as saying that "the Son of Man came not to be served but to serve and give his life as a ransom for many" (the Greek word used suggests in the place of). Another key verse is from Paul's correspondence with the Church in Corinth, his second letter and chapter 5 where he writes "him who knew no sin he made to be sin on our behalf [a different preposition from the one used in Mark 10, 45 but many Evangelicals argue that the preposition also carries the sense of in place of, substitution] in order that we might become the righteousness of God in him". An important Old Testament passage is the account of the action by the High Priest on the day of atonement involving a goat. In Leviticus 16, 21 we read this: "Aaron is to lay both hands on the head of the live goat and confess over it all the wickedness and rebellion of the Israelites – all their sins – and put them on the goat's head." This is the origin of our English expression "a scape goat".

Another significant Old Testament passage that is picked up in the gospels and other parts of the New Testament to throw light on the significance of Christ's death on the cross and the significance of the bread and wine in the Eucharist is what is recorded in Exodus as taking place on the final night of the Israelites in Egypt. One final judgement was to fall on every Egyptian household; the angel of death would cause the death of every eldest son; the Israelites were to sacrifice a lamb and take some of its blood and smear it on the lintels of their doors. When the angel of death saw the blood, the angel would pass over that home and the family would be protected from death by the shed blood of the sacrificial lamb. As John the Baptist encounters Jesus as recorded in John's gospel he says: "Behold the Lamb of God." In John's gospel Jesus dies on the cross as the Passover lambs are being sacrificed. In the Synoptic gospels the last meal Jesus shares with his disciples is a Passover meal investing the bread and wine with new significance associated with Jesus's forthcoming death on the cross. Whichever timeline we follow, that of John or that of the Synoptic gospels, there is a very clear link with the Passover.

Another key passage from the Old Testament that is picked up in the New Testament to shed light on the significance of the cross is from the so-called Suffering Servant Song in Isaiah 53, words again that were helpfully picked up and set to evocative music in Handel's *Messiah*, the suffering servant suffers in our place and "by his stripes we have been healed".

John Stott published in 1986 a magisterial treatment of the significance of Christ's death on the cross, simply titled *The Cross of Christ* (IVP 1986). He has a chapter on the problem of forgiveness, dealing with issues such as the gravity of sin, God's holiness and his wrath. There is a chapter on "Satisfaction for sin" which among other topics explores satisfying God's honour and justice, referring to Archbishop Anselm's major theological treatise titled *Cur Deus Homo*, holding together God's love and holiness. There is a chapter on the "Self-substitution of God" that has quite a lot on sacrifice in the Old Testament and how that relates to Jesus's self-sacrifice. In a chapter on "The Achievement of the Cross" Stott explores biblical concepts of propitiation (rather than expiation which many modern translations of the Bible prefer), redemption (slave-market imagery), justification (law-court imagery), reconciliation. There is a chapter on the cross as "The Revelation of God", revealing God's glory (John 12 and 17), God's justice, the love of God, exercising a moral influence. In another chapter he explores a perspective on the cross which was popular among the early Fathers and popularised by Gustav Aulen in *Christus Victor*, namely the conquest of evil, imagery found in Colossians 2, 15. His book was published in Swedish in 1930 and an English translation came out in 1931. He identified three main interpretations of the significance of the Cross: what he called the "objective view" or "satisfaction" later developed within Evangelical theology as penal substitution; the subjective view or Christ's death on the cross exercising a moral influence on us, a view especially put forward by Peter Abelard in opposition to Anselm's focus on the "satisfaction" view of the cross; and the third view which he described as the "Classic" view (also known as the Ransom theory) of Christ triumphing at the cross over Satan and all the powers of evil; Aulen argued that this was the view held by the vast majority of the early Church Fathers and was the predominant view for the first thousand years of the Church.

Stott acknowledges that there is a rich variety of images of the significance of the cross in the pages of the New Testament and also drawing on Old Testament imagery but argues that the predominant and controlling image is that of substitutionary atonement. That is my own view and I believe there is spiritual power in preaching it and this has characterised Evangelical doctrine and spirituality historically. However, more recently a significant number of Evangelicals have expressed unhappiness with the doctrine of substitutionary atonement. The Director of Ordinands I worked with latterly as Bishop of Tewkesbury made a point of pushing Evangelical ordinands strongly on the issue regarding it as an immoral doctrine. I recall too, a conversation with Michael Perham my diocesan bishop coming away from a service where we had sung the renewal song "How deep the Father's love" that contains the words "The Father turns his face away"; Michael couldn't understand those words theologically. Also, when the hymn "In Christ alone" was sung in Gloucester Cathedral in my time, the line in verse 2 "the wrath of God was satisfied" was replaced with the words "the love of God was magnified". Interestingly, when Archbishop Justin Welby chose "in Christ alone" at his consecration, the original words of the hymn were used. It is true that some Victorian Evangelical preaching drove an unhelpful wedge between a wrathful Father God and a loving Son which is difficult to square with the words of Paul in 2 Corinthians 5 that "God was in Christ reconciling the world to himself". However, for me these words take us to an issue that is central to our understanding of the cross, that at the cross the claims of God's justice and holiness are fully met at the same time as the claims of his boundless love for sinful humanity. Also, this perspective helps us make some sense of the cry of dereliction recorded in Mark 15, 34: "My God, my God, why have you forsaken/abandoned me?"

Though as an Evangelical, I warm to the doctrine of substitutionary atonement as being an important strand in sharing the gospel, as an Anglican I acknowledge the rich variety of perspectives and imagery found in the pages of the New Testament to shed light on the significance of the cross. I also have some sympathy with Maurice Wiles's reflection that the various doctrines of the cross are valuable in exploring the significance of the cross but if followed too dogmatically to explain what is taking place at the cross, are more likely to appal than to appeal.

At the heart of Christian faith unifying the different traditions within Anglicanism is the idea of a personal encounter with Christ. For Evangelicals encounter with Christ is above all through engagement with Scripture and with the message of the Bible. For Anglo-Catholics encounter with Christ is above all through the sacramental and priestly life of the church. For Charismatics the encounter with Christ is focused especially on a dynamic experience of the work of the Holy Spirit in one's life. For those in a Liberal tradition it can be about encountering Christ as one works with and among the poor, the hungry, those in prison, engaging with social need in all its variety, in the light of the parable of the Sheep and the Goats in Matthew chapter 25.

Over the years I have come to believe that there is a rich variety of ways in which people may encounter Christ and that such a belief marks me out as an Anglican Evangelical as opposed to being an Evangelical in a more Free Church tradition. This has become a growing conviction over many years in ministry, though even in my more Conservative Evangelical days at Cambridge, I recall feeling very unhappy with the fact that some of my Roman Catholic friends were not allowed as Roman Catholics to belong to CICCU and strongly disagreeing with some of my CICCU friends who wrote off Roman Catholics as non-Christians. Interestingly, David Watson who was a leader in the Charismatic movement in the Church of England when Vicar of St Michael-le-Belfry, York, was heavily criticised by many Evangelicals for working alongside Roman Catholics in mission and seeing them as definite Christians. He believed he couldn't fail to acknowledge a significant work of the Holy Spirit in renewal in many Roman Catholic churches.

Focus on Evangelism as an Archdeacon and as a Suffragan Bishop

In 1980 I was invited by Michael Adie, Bishop of Guildford, to be Archdeacon of Surrey. As Evangelicals made an increasingly significant contribution to the life of the Church of England, a number of bishops felt it was important to include an Evangelical on their Senior Team. So it was my privilege to serve as the "token" Evangelical on the Bishop of Guildford's Senior Staff. An archdeacon in the Church of England is expected to serve as "the eyes and ears" of the Diocesan Bishop. Inevitably, the role involved sitting on a very large number of committees and keeping the bishop informed about various areas of diocesan life. However, there was also opportunity to carve out a distinctive ministry shaped by one's own interests and emphases in ministry. My time as archdeacon coincided with the Decade of Evangelism and I had the privilege of working in partnership with Canon Mavis Wilson, the Diocesan Missioner. She encouraged me to write to a number of clergy across the diocese to invite them to consider recommending one or more of their lay people to join her and me as part of a Faith-Sharing initiative. As an archdeacon I needed to be seen to be available to all parishes whatever their theological outlook, Evangelical, Anglo-Catholic, Liberal, Charismatic or good old "middle of the road" Anglican. The lay people who joined our Faith-Sharing team whatever the theological ethos of their parish church interestingly tended to be people who were on the more Evangelical spectrum. Interestingly, as Christians move around the country some who are Evangelical will look for a Church that is clearly Evangelical and not be concerned whether it is Anglican or Baptist or Methodist or Independent. Others, however, as Evangelicals see themselves as standing in an Anglican tradition and so will attend their local parish church whether or not it is Evangelical. I found as I travelled round the diocese both as an archdeacon and later as a bishop that most parish churches which were not openly Evangelical included within their congregation quite a number of people who would describe themselves as Evangelical.

We undertook some basic training for the team members and then I wrote to a number of clergy encouraging them to consider having members of the team for a weekend or a week-long focus on sharing faith. A selling-point was that the team was made up of very ordinary lay people, no different from the church members we were sharing with over the weekend or the week. One church member at the end of a weekend of faith sharing commented "your team members are just like us!" I answered him by saying that was indeed the point and if our team members could share their faith in a relaxed and informal way what was to stop him and other members of his congregation doing the same?

When I became Bishop of Tewkesbury it seemed to be natural to introduce Faith-Sharing teams to Gloucester diocese. My own understanding of the role of a bishop includes a teaching ministry, a pastoral ministry and being a leader in evangelism and mission.

One selling point of the Faith-Sharing initiative was that we made it clear that the clergy and PCC could be in charge of designing the kind of events undertaken by the team. This led to us embarking on what proved to be a particularly popular model in the multi-parish benefices of Gloucester diocese. One vicar of a multi-parish benefice I approached about bringing in my Faith-Sharing team told me that "it wasn't his kind of thing!" I encouraged him to ponder on it and he came back to me after a while and said he would be very happy for me to bring a team to his group of parishes provided he could decide the shape of the weekend. He came up with a Pilgrimage model involving the team in walking round the area of the benefice with members of the local congregations and stopping at each of the churches in turn and having a short act of worship and having one of our team members talk briefly about their own faith journey. The vicar's wife was very involved with Riding for the Disabled and brought one of her donkeys on the pilgrimage round the different parishes. That proved quite challenging every time we reached a style on our pilgrimage walk!

One unexpected benefit of the Faith-Sharing initiative was that about half of the original members of my team in Gloucester diocese went on to train for ordination having discovered a new-found confidence in their Christian faith and in wanting to share their faith with others.

Chapter 7

Understanding Mission on a Broad Canvas

The Lausanne Conferences and Holistic Mission

In the previous chapter I made passing reference to the significance of the Lausanne Conferences in causing many Evangelicals to come to understand Mission in holistic terms rather than simply as equivalent to Evangelism. Moving in Evangelical circles, I was aware that many Evangelicals viewed those who majored on a "social gospel" with great suspicion. As Evangelicals gathered at Lausanne on a number of occasions, especially through John Stott's leadership, rather than seeing a division between personal salvation and the socio-political implications of the gospel these came to be viewed as two equally important strands in a fully rounded understanding of the gospel. John Stott was largely responsible for drafting the Lausanne Covenant of 1974. A key emphasis was the recognition of social justice being a clear biblical responsibility for Evangelical Christians, not set in opposition to personal salvation but going hand in hand with personal salvation, both equally important.

Oxford diocese during Lent, 2023, offered daily reflections with the title "Come and See". The reflections were based on the Beatitudes as found in Matthew's gospel chapter 5 and including the Beatitude "Blessed are those who hunger and thirst after righteousness". The reflections showed how each Beatitude is exemplified in the life and ministry of Jesus and forms a challenge to disciples to imitate the example of Jesus. Luke, in his gospel, presents Jesus preaching his first sermon in the synagogue in Nazareth on Isaiah 61, a manifesto for his own ministry; the passage has a spiritual dimension to it but also very clearly a practical dimension to bring about a more just world. There are many passages in the Old Testament especially in the Prophets which focus on God's passion for justice, righteousness, compassion. There are three particularly vulnerable people who are singled out on many occasions as the object of God's special care and therefore to be shown care by God's people, namely the widow, the orphan and the stranger in your midst – a challenge in our contemporary world about how we respond to the plight of refugees. During Lent, the passage of Scripture appointed each day for Night Prayer was from Isaiah 58 and offered the following challenge, again a broad vision of mission:

> Is not this the fast that I choose: to loose the bonds of injustice, to undo the thongs of the yoke, to let the oppressed go free, and to break every yoke? Is it not to share your bread with the hungry, and bring the homeless poor into your house; when you see the naked, to cover them, and not to hide yourself from your own kin?

Norman Thomas in *Readings in World Mission* in a section titled "Evangelicals and the whole gospel" introduces the section with a quote "God is equally interested in our service and in our evangelistic task" and reflects on the make-up of participants at the 1974 Lausanne Congress:

> The majority among the 2,480 evangelical participants from 150 countries ... were conservative in theology and Western in outlook. However, among the more than 1000 Third World participants, a new Evangelical voice was to be heard. At Lausanne two young Latin American Evangelicals argued against the separation of evangelism and social concern. Samuel Escobar, a Peruvian, warned Evangelicals to avoid the temptation of reducing the gospel to a spirituality without discipleship.

Then secretary of the Intervarsity Christian Fellowship of Canada, he was soon to move to Argentina as president of the Latin American Theological Fraternity. Next, Rene Padilla, associate general secretary of the International Fellowship of Evangelical Students in Buenos Aires, denounced the "cultural Christianity" associated with the American way of life as being as harmful to the Gospel as secular Christianity. Together with others of the Evangelical "left" they succeeded in securing in the Lausanne Covenant an affirmation that "evangelism and socio-political involvement are both parts of our Christian duty".[9]

Thomas goes on to give some quotes from Samuel Escobar's "Evangelism and Man's Search for Freedom, Justice and Fulfilment in Is Revolution Change?"

> Christian service is not optional. It is not something we can do if we want to. It is the mark of the new life; "You will know them by their fruits." "If you love me, you will keep my commandments." If we are in Christ we have the spirit of service of Christ. So to discuss whether we should evangelise or promote social action is worthless. They go together. They are inseparable. One without the other is evidence of a deficient Christian life. So we must not try to justify service for our neighbour by claiming that it will "help us" in our evangelism. God is equally interested in our service and in our evangelistic task. Let us not have a guilty conscience over our schools, hospitals, health centres, student centres, and so on. If they are also used for evangelism, splendid! But let us not use them as a medium of coercion to force the gospel on others. It is not necessary. In themselves they are an expression of Christian maturity.... It is fundamental

to recognise that society is more than just the sum of a number of individuals. It is naïve to affirm that all that is needed is new persons in order to have a new society.[10]

This takes us back to the inadequacy of the illustration I referred to which was used by my training incumbent of the little boy and the jigsaw with a picture of the world on one side of the jigsaw pieces and a picture of a human being on the other side of the pieces!

John Stott is quoted in David Bosch's magisterial work *Transforming Mission: Paradigm Shifts in Theology of Mission*, "I now see more clearly that not only the consequences of the commission (Matthew 28) but the actual commission itself must be understood to include social as well as evangelistic responsibility, unless we are to be guilty of distorting the words of Jesus."[11] However, Bosch argues that the Congress and the Covenant continued to operate in terms of the two-mandate approach and within that to uphold the priority of evangelism. The Covenant explicitly stated that "reconciliation with man [sic] is not reconciliation with God nor is social action evangelism nor is political liberation salvation". Bosch argues that it was only later that the view expressed above by John Stott became more widely and fully accepted. Bosch goes on to quote the Wheaton declaration of 1983: "Evil is not only in the human heart but also in social structures. The Mission of the Church includes both the proclamation of the Gospel and its demonstration. We must therefore evangelise, respond to human needs and press for social transformation."[12]

TEAR Fund Founded in 1968

Evidence of Evangelicals taking social justice seriously was indicated in the founding of TEAR Fund by the Revd George Hoffman in 1968 (this evolved from the Evangelical Alliance Relief Fund of the early 1960s). Though TEAR Fund has always been inter-denominational, it is not insignificant that it was an Anglican Evangelical clergyman, George Hoffman, who played a key role in the setting up of TEAR Fund one year after the Keele Congress. TEAR Fund offered devotional reflections online for each day of Lent, 2023, and the reflection for Wednesday 15 March was headed: Who is responsible? Their broad mission agenda includes care for creation. They quote Genesis 1, 26 in the New Living Translation: "They (human beings) will reign over the fish in the sea, the birds in the sky, the livestock, all the wild animals on the earth." The reflection went on as follows: "Humanity's calling from the beginning has been to 'reign' over creation. But before we get ideas above our station, we should remember that we are to reign God's way, as servants. We are to serve and care for the fish, birds, plants ... all our global neighbours." TEAR fund is involved in every part of the world working alongside local partners to bring about a more just, more compassionate world.

Holistic Mission Increasingly on the Agenda

One significant shift among many Anglican Evangelicals during the second part of the twentieth century (a shift which I personally came to embrace enthusiastically) then was the acknowledgement of the importance of a holistic approach to mission that includes evangelism alongside social and political involvement, working for a more just world and to challenge unjust structure wherever they are to be found and work towards their transformation. Many Evangelical Anglicans have embraced the five marks of Mission adopted by the Anglican Consultative Council in 1984.

As Bishop of Tewkesbury, I was sponsoring bishop for those seeking to explore a vocation to ordained ministry. I played my part alongside the Diocesan Director of Ordinands (DDO) in preparing potential candidates for a BAP (Bishops' Advisory Panel). The DDO and I always ensured that before potential candidates attended a BAP they were familiar with those five marks of Mission: "To proclaim the Good News of the Kingdom; to teach, baptise and nurture new believers; to respond to human need by loving service; to seek to transform unjust structures of society; to challenge violence of every kind and to pursue peace and reconciliation; to safeguard the integrity of creation and renew the life of the earth." The words "to challenge violence of every kind and to pursue peace and reconciliation" were only added later in 2012.

Mission is the all-embracing big picture of God's grand plan for his creation; within that evangelism is the specific task of sharing the gospel and enabling individuals to become followers of Jesus. During my time at Theological College and during my curacy at Emmanuel, Northwood, I was working with the model of the boy and the jigsaw. I believed that the key task entrusted to the Church by the risen Christ was to preach the good news of personal salvation through Christ's finished work of redemption on the cross and as people responded to that good news and became followers of Jesus Christ, so areas of society impacted by them would begin to be transformed to reflect more of God's Kingly rule. At that time I did not have an holistic understanding of mission as reflected in the five marks of mission and tended to equate mission and evangelism.

It was during my time as Vicar of Holy Trinity, Margate, when I was still initially tending to equate mission and evangelism and understand mission in terms of personal salvation that I began to recognise the importance of a more holistic approach to mission through becoming aware of structures within society that made it very difficult for some people to flourish as human beings, and as a result finding it very difficult to be open to making a personal response to the preaching of the gospel. Margate was very mixed socially. On some farming land opposite the church a new council estate was built; the vision for the estate was that people who had worked for the council and others in the community might pay more to live in a really high quality council house. The first 50 or so houses were occupied by such tenants but the remaining almost 600 houses remained unfilled and people with various social needs ended up being housed. It was a time when some of the Vietnamese Boat People were being settled in Thanet and some Vietnamese families were duly housed. As a Church we sought to respond to a variety of social needs on this new estate working in partnership with Social Services. Initially, they were wary of partnering with a Christian Church but came to recognise that we could be trusted and increasingly allowed us to get involved with many families on our own without interference from Social Services.

I referred in an earlier chapter to the building of a Church Lounge and the congregation member who took responsibility for the lounge with an impressive group of helpers had a clear vision linked with boundless energy for engaging with the wider community ensuring a welcoming presence including meals, support groups for single parents and for people out of work and a number of other areas of need.

As Bishop of Tewkesbury, I was aware of ministering in an area of the country that contained a lot of wealth and privilege. However, there were pockets of deprivation in parts of the diocese and homelessness was an issue not only in Gloucester itself but also surprisingly in parts of Cheltenham. I discovered that as a bishop it was possible to take initiatives and draw in others to work with me. Working with the Director of Social Responsibility, I organised three Sleep-outs as a way of flagging up the issue of homelessness and also raising funds for charities working with the homeless. We involved a lot of young people across the diocese in the Sleep-out. The first year the plan had been that they would also sleep but of course they didn't! So for the following two Sleep-outs activities were organised for the young people to keep them awake all night learning more about issues related to homelessness. One of my daughters-in-law commissioned a play about homelessness and produced it three times during the course of the night with different groups of young people. As a bishop I was able to approach local MPs and Chairmen of Councils challenging them to join me in the Sleep-out and a number did. The woman MP for the Forest of Dean at the time dined out for quite some time on her claim that she "had slept with the Bishop of Tewkesbury"!

Many Church of England dioceses over the years forged links with dioceses in other parts of the Anglican Communion. For various reasons Gloucester diocese had never forged a link. Bishop David Bentley was keen that we should forge a link and the two of us after consulting with others agreed that a link with two dioceses in India would be helpful. At the time I was on the UK Council of World Vision and as a Council member was asked to visit some World Vision projects in India together with my wife. This was particularly attractive to us as my wife had been born in Bangalore in India as her family had lived in India for several generations with both her grandfathers working as surgeons in the Indian army.

During our links with India, I became aware that an important part of Christian mission in India involved schools, hostels and hospitals, displaying Christian compassion at a very practical level. Though many did embrace Christian faith through sharing in the life of hostels and schools and receiving treatment in a Christian hospital, Indian Christians were clear that involvement in these areas was not seen as a means to evangelise but undertaken in the name of Christ as an expression of God's compassionate love for a needy world.

We were eventually as a diocese encouraged to develop links with Karnataka Central diocese (including Bangalore) where Bishop Vasanthakumar was bishop and with Dornakal diocese in Andhra Pradesh, a largely urban diocese and a deeply rural diocese. Dornakal was the first Indian diocese to have an Indian bishop, Azariah, who was deeply committed to the unity of the Church and played a significant part in laying the foundations for the emergence of the United Church of South India which took place on 27 September, 1947, in the Cathedral in Madras – a significant milestone in the history of the Ecumenical Movement. Interestingly, one of our Wycliffe Hall Students, Sue Billington-Harper, a Rhodes Scholar from the States, while based at Wycliffe Hall, wrote her Oxford DPhil on Bishop Azariah and later published her thesis in a very readable book titled *In the Shadow of the Mahatma*.

Many young people in Gloucester diocese came from very privileged backgrounds and a positive strand in the link was to send out a group of young people every summer to experience life in both dioceses. This proved to be a life-transforming experience for many of the young people.

Evangelicals and Ecological Issues: A Rocha

Evangelicals have been accused of only being interested in people's personal salvation, preparing people for eternity and not being concerned about the transformation of this world to reflect God's justice and compassion. Historically, Christians generally were slow to wake up to important ecological issues. In the USA there is a movement of Evangelical Environmentalists who drawing on the account of creation in Genesis have emphasised the role of human beings in being responsible stewards of God's creation. Too often in the past Christians were inclined to assume that the command to "subdue the earth" was a licence to waste the earth's resources in an irresponsible way. Among other issues they are committed with others to taking climate change seriously and taking necessary steps to reverse climate warming.

Peter and Miranda Harris founded A Rocha in 1983, a specifically Christian organisation committed to caring for God's creation. Its website describes it as a global family of conservation organisations working together to live out God's calling to care for creation and to equip others to do likewise. It is a specifically Christian organisation and has been largely driven by Anglican Evangelical Christians. ECO Church began as an A Rocha project in the UK in 2016 and has proved very effective in inspiring and encouraging local churches to take the care of God's creation seriously in every area of church life. Initially taking root in churches in England and Wales, it has spread as a movement to many other parts of the world. It is one significant example of Evangelical Christians embracing a much broader understanding of mission. There is a very clear biblical mandate found in the creation injunction to human beings to exercise a responsible stewardship of God's good creation. Sadly, the use of the word "subdue" in Genesis for many centuries encouraged Christians to believe they could abuse creation for their own ends and Christians were slow to take on board a sense of responsible stewardship. A biblical mandate is also found in the vision spelt out in the eighth chapter of Paul's letter to the Romans that "the creation itself will be liberated from its bondage to decay and brought into the glorious freedom of the children of God".

The Church of England, as already mentioned, has along with other denominations committed itself unreservedly to the five marks of mission and those five marks present us with a holistic understanding of mission that reflects the priorities and concerns of the heart of God that were displayed in the life and ministry of Jesus and become a challenging manifesto for followers of Jesus to live out individually and corporately.

Chapter 8

Sacred Space and Holy Places

The Significance of a Sabbatical in the Holy Land

I have referred to my Sabbatical at Tantur in Jerusalem and its significance in shaping my theological and ecclesiological outlook. As I embarked on my Sabbatical in January, 1994, I was very sceptical about holy places. Up to that time I had had no particular longing to visit the Holy Land on pilgrimage. I took my stand on Jesus's final promise to his followers at the end of Matthew's gospel: "Lo I am with you always to the end of the age." I held to a view that as disciples of Christ we can meet with the risen Lord anywhere at any time and do not need special buildings or special places. I often referred to the fact that for the first three centuries, Christians had no special buildings and yet that was a time of enormous growth for the Christian Church.

I found my views deeply challenged by my three months at Tantur. The chapel where we gathered both for a daily midday Eucharist and for informal evening worship became an increasingly special place of encounter together with the other participants on the course from very different theological and church backgrounds. It became a "holy place".

During the three-month course, trips were organised to the various "holy places" including three days spent by Lake Galilee. Amongst other places, my wife and I found the beautiful Church of the Beatitudes was a place of deep encounter with Christ as we spent time in meditation on the Beatitudes beautifully inscribed on the walls, by the windows looking out over Lake Galilee and on the ceiling. Another special place was the little chapel by the Lake commemorating the site where the risen Christ met with his disciples as recorded in John 21.

In Jerusalem itself four places became particularly special to my wife and myself. The Crusader Church of St Anne at the Pool of Bethesda, the Church of the Holy Sepulchre, Dominus Flevit Church designed beautifully in the shape of a teardrop by the Italian architect Antonio Barluzzi and the Church of All Nations in the Garden of Gethsemane. All four of these churches over many visits became special places for us both of a deep sense of encounter with the risen Christ. It became increasingly difficult to deny the reality of holy places, places of special encounter with Christ, in the language of Celtic spirituality "thin places", where the boundary between this world and the heavenly realm, between time and eternity is especially "thin".

My wife found the experience of three months in the Holy Land especially enriching spiritually and was inspired to write quite a number of poems capturing both the pain of the deeply divided land but also the sense of Christ's presence. The following poem she wrote for one of our evening services at Tantur and one of the Notre Dame University students at Tantur with us did an evocative dance acting out the message of the poem:

In this place
Worship and call;
Invoke to God Almighty
In transcendent tones
This memory's yearning
That draws our Lord beyond time
Here.
And you,
O Jesus,
Bending low
Can scoop our worships at your call.
Then we, and all creation,
Court time together

In memorial space
Lingering, hovering
To know God's awe
And all mysterious majesty
In this place.

Another poem was inspired by time spent in Dominus Flevit Church on the Mount of Olives and after the tragic massacre of Muslim worshippers in the mosque in Hebron on a Friday at the end of February 1994:

Your place of tears is here.
You see the sharp nails
Pierced through and through
Like glass, spiked, sharp.
Unforgiving, in the pain
Which You feel even now.
Your blood mingled with Your tears
Runs down to the ground
In rivulets of amber, red and gold
Opening up channels in the earth below
And around our feet.
I see the blood.
I see the tears.[13]

Gloucester Diocese and Holy Places

My coming to appreciate holy space and holy places was strengthened especially during my time as Bishop of Tewkesbury in Gloucester diocese with its 400 churches, many of them Grade 1 listed. As Bishop of Tewkesbury, I was privileged to have a special relationship with Tewkesbury Abbey. My first Christmas in the diocese, Michael Tavinor, the vicar (later on to be Dean of Hereford Cathedral) invited me to preach at Midnight Mass. The family were staying with us and came along to the service and were amused to see me disappear during the service behind clouds of incense from not just one censer but two censers! On several occasions we took friends to Tewkesbury Abbey. After the 1998 Lambeth Conference, the Bishop of Nevada and his wife with whom we had become friends during the Conference came to stay overnight with us and we took them to the Abbey. As we entered the Abbey the bishop's wife stood rooted to the ground, tears streaming down her cheeks and she commented: "I cannot get over how immensely holy this place is!" As Jacob in Genesis after his dream of a ladder reaching from earth to heaven exclaimed: "Surely the Lord is in this place." I had been resistant to the idea of holy places ignoring the many places in the Old Testament especially where the idea of holy space, holy places, is there for those with the eyes to see.

During my time in Gloucester diocese, Tewkesbury Abbey always remained a special place for me, but there were many other churches especially throughout the Cotswolds where I was privileged to preach and preside at the Eucharist where again I had a strong sense of standing on holy ground. In part I sense it was because of the worship and prayers of faithful Christians down many centuries, but more than that a sense that the living Lord chooses to honour those places with a special sense of his presence.

The Church of South India and Holy Space

As mentioned in the previous chapter, as Bishop of Tewkesbury I helped to develop a link between Gloucester diocese and two dioceses in the Church of South India, Karnataka Central, centred on Bangalore, and Dornakal in Andhra Pradesh. My wife had been born in Bangalore as her family was there for several generations and only returned to England at the time of the Partition. We had never visited India so it was a privilege to develop the diocesan link. Our first visit to India was with World Vision (I was on their UK Board at the time) and we were able to visit World Vision projects in Kerala, Vijayawada, Calcutta and Delhi. We especially became good friends with Vasanthakumar, Bishop of Karnataka Central diocese, and his wife, Nirmala, who was ordained. Later, I was privileged to spend a second Sabbatical based in Bangalore and made use of the excellent resources of the ecumenical library at the United Theological College in Bangalore. I found myself deeply moved by the way that Indian pastors always took off their shoes leaving them in the vestry as they went into church to lead worship and I was expected similarly to remove my shoes and go barefoot. Again, with recollection of the Lord saying to Moses in Exodus 3 "take off your shoes for you are standing on holy ground" going barefoot fostered a strong sense of standing on holy ground to worship the living God.

Jesus in conversation with the Samaritan woman at the well about whether Jerusalem was the correct place to worship God stated that God is Spirit and we must worship him in Spirit and in Truth. However, some buildings help us to worship God in Spirit and in Truth. Some places where in the words of T S Eliot "prayer has been valid", is where prayer has been soaked into the very fabric of the church. Eliot found such a place in the hamlet of Little Gidding, in Cambridgeshire; for him it was a numinous place, filled with a sense of the presence of the living God. This tiny hamlet was the home of a religious community founded in 1626 by Nicholas Farrar and two of his siblings and their extended families; so the tiny community was soaked in prayer over a few hundred years.[14]

The Impact of Covid Lockdown on Holy Space

During lockdown in the wake of the Covid pandemic being unable to meet in Church for several months questions were raised about whether sacred space and holy places were particularly important. As mentioned before, in retirement my wife and I have chosen to be linked with a church that would describe itself as in the Liberal Catholic tradition. It is a multicultural congregation embracing people from many different parts of the world. In such a culturally mixed congregation there are inevitably significantly different theological outlooks. The vicar helpfully holds together in a very Anglican way both a focus on good biblical preaching and a focus on the central importance of the Eucharist. During lockdown like most churches we began to meet online, many of us sharing in a service streamed on Zoom and also made available on Facebook. Our Vicar was not happy with the idea of celebrating the Eucharist on her own and not happy with the practice of some clergy of encouraging people in their own homes to set aside bread and wine and to communicate themselves in that way. So all of our online services with the exception of Christmas and Easter Sunday were non-eucharistic. They were services of the Word. Towards the end of each service, our vicar used the following helpful prayer incorporating the prayer of Richard of Chichester: "Thanks be to you Lord Jesus Christ, for all the benefits you have given me, for all the pains and insults you have borne for me; since we cannot now receive you in the sacrament we ask you to come spiritually into our hearts [at this point she would pause for a good 40 seconds for silent prayerful reflection] O most merciful Redeemer, Friend and Brother, may I know you more clearly, love you more dearly and follow you more nearly day by day."

Though my faith on a daily basis is nurtured and deepened through engagement with scripture, I found myself missing the Eucharist greatly and because I am ordained, I did celebrate the Eucharist for myself and my wife on a fortnightly basis usually on a Monday morning incorporating Morning Prayer as well. Interestingly, our vicar didn't feel she should receive communion herself while her congregation members were deprived of the sacrament. The eucharistic celebrations that my wife and I shared in during lockdown were for us both very special moments of encounter with the crucified and risen Christ. However, though we were aware of the presence of Christ with us in the intimacy of our flat we both greatly missed being in the Church building as sacred space and enjoying fellowship with other Christians. Even as lockdown eased and we began to meet back in Church (though a number of members of the congregation were uncomfortable attending services because of Covid and being personally vulnerable), we missed sharing the peace (we simply used sign language to share the peace at a safe distance) and we didn't have coffee after the service. As I explored in my opening chapter the majority of the 100 or so models of Church, Paul Minear identified in his *Images of the Church in the New Testament* majored on personal relationship with other Christians as central to our understanding of and experience of Church. Covid deprived us sadly of warm fellowship.

Archbishop Justin Welby during lockdown presided at a Eucharist on Easter Sunday from his kitchen table. I was certainly not the only person to wonder whether this Eucharist was less "special" because it was celebrated from an ordinary secular space. When our vicar streamed services from the vicarage during lockdown she took care to create a sense of sacred space. For example, during the Epiphany season she had a beautiful nativity scene in the background and during the Easter season an empty tomb and always a lit candle which she drew attention to as a reminder of Christ's presence with us as the light of the world.

There was an interesting story in *The Telegraph* on 3 June, 2021, about a Roman Catholic priest, Father Len Black of Inverness. He was a finalist in the competition run by Cuprinol Wood for imaginative use of sheds! During lockdown he streamed Mass from his garden shed. Roman Catholics and non-Catholics from across the world including some as far away as a drilling platform in the South Atlantic joined in online. Some non-Catholics as a result showed interest in becoming Roman Catholics having been able to experience worship outside the formality of a church building.

In the Jewish tradition the Temple featured as a holy place and God's presence was very closely associated with the Temple. This was the setting for Isaiah's overwhelming vision of the majesty and holiness of God. However, there was also a strand found in the prophetic tradition that questioned over-reliance on the assurance of God's presence in the physical space of the Temple. For over 200 years the first Christians had no special buildings. Jesus in his conversation with the Samaritan woman at the well in John 4 suggests that the most significant thing in worship is not a particular place but worship that is in Spirit and in Truth. As mentioned in an earlier chapter John's account of the Cleansing of the Temple, unlike the Synoptic gospels, is placed at the start of Jesus's ministry and when challenged by the religious leaders, Jesus makes the following statement: "Destroy this Temple and I will raise it again in three days." John goes on to comment that Jesus was referring to the Temple of his body. For John it seems that the risen Christ will take the place of the Jewish Temple. John points to an understanding of the Church as a community of men and women, young people and children gathered round the risen Christ. Not a building but a community. The Synoptic gospels also record Jesus saying that where two or three are gathered together in his name, there he is in their midst.

Though I believe that the main focus of the New Testament's understanding of Church is on community and relationship, Luke in Acts conveys the impression that the early Christians as well as meeting informally in each other's homes continued to meet in the Temple and in the Synagogue. Their worship seems to have been influenced by the pattern of Synagogue worship too. The reason why the early Christians didn't have special buildings was probably largely dictated by practical factors (as a persecuted minority group) rather than by any theological factors and once under the Emperor Constantine Christianity became the officially recognised religion of the Roman Empire church buildings sprang up across the Empire. Church buildings continued to be significant for Christian worship down the centuries (again as an Anglican Evangelical I recognise the place of Tradition alongside Scripture as influencing our practice as Christians) except where as a result of persecution (for example, in China in the twentieth century) the Church went underground and not only survived but flourished through informal cell groups.

In the *Church Times* of 28 May, 2021, there was a book review of *Women of the Catacombs: Memoirs of the Underground Orthodox Church in Stalin's Russia* by Wallace L Daniel, editor and translator. Soviet propaganda argued that religion would become a thing of the past, but it didn't in Russia; the reviewer argues that the fact that Christianity not simply survived but flourished was largely due to the lives and faith of those whose memoirs are recorded in this book. Forbidden to meet openly in church buildings they met in secret, part of the underground church and their courageous and attractive faith led to many being converted to Christianity. As in China so in Russia, during years of persecution the Christian Church continued to flourish through cells, the basis of all life.

In the same *Church Times* there was an interview with Eileen Eggington whom I knew from my curacy days in Emmanuel, Northwood. As mentioned in an earlier chapter we used to take six vans of young people for a Christian holiday on the continent each summer and one year when I was one of the drivers, Eileen was one of the "mums" who shared in the spiritual and practical leadership for the young people. Eileen is the project officer for the Malawi Association for Christian Support. In the interview she spoke of her experience of visiting Malawi on several occasions. Sixty per cent of the population are Christian and about 10% are Anglicans. She spoke of some meeting in well-built churches while others still gather in the open air under a tree for their worship. Who is to say, she asked, that the group meeting under a tree for worship are less a church than Christians meeting in the finest cathedral in England. As so often with the Anglican Church it is not either/or but both/and.

Reflecting on those Continental Holidays, one place we visited twice in my time was Vastervik in Sweden. The campsite had a candle-lit chapel where we gathered every evening for worship and a talk. I have very special memories of open-air Eucharists by a lakeside surrounded by glorious scenery, but those evening worship times in the candle-lit chapel, sacred space, holy place, were very special too.

Has the experience of online worship during the pandemic raised questions about the need for specially dedicated, consecrated buildings? When I was Bishop of Tewkesbury, I would quite often when talking with Church members remind them that though the 400 churches in the diocese, many of them glorious Grade 1 listed buildings, were a reminder of the vibrancy of Christian faith at the heart of rural and urban communities, every single church building could be destroyed, but the Church of Jesus Christ would survive in the lives of his disciples.

Different Theological Responses to Sharing in Communion at Home during Lockdown

A survey carried out by Leslie Francis and Andrew Village revealed interesting responses among clergy and laity of different theological persuasions. In response to a question as to whether it was right for clergy to celebrate Communion alone in their own homes without broadcasting the service to others, 50% of Anglo-Catholic clergy and 46% of Anglo-Catholic laity believed it was acceptable while only 12% of Evangelical clergy believed it was acceptable though 31% of Evangelical laity were happy with the idea. Another question was whether it was right for people in their own homes to receive communion from their own bread and wine as part of an online communion service; only 18% of Anglo-Catholic clergy and 26% of Anglo-Catholic laity found that acceptable, while 41% of Evangelical clergy and 62% of Evangelical laity found that practice acceptable.

When I was Vicar of Holy Trinity, Margate, I would have described myself still as Conservative Evangelical (more in a Free Church tradition than a distinctively Anglican tradition though during the eight and half years I was vicar there, I moved in a more distinctively Anglican direction in my theology and practice). On one occasion the curate and myself (bad planning!) were both away on holiday at the same time and a Communion service needed covering. At that time we had recently started employing a lay pastor full time who was greatly loved by the four congregations that made up the church. As a law-abiding Anglican priest, I brought in a neighbouring priest to preside at the Communion Service. He was not known to any of the congregation and many of the lay people (especially those new to Christian faith) could not understand why our lay pastor whom they knew and loved could not preside and why someone from outside had to be brought in who was not known to any congregation members. Though I was happy to be canonically obedient, I did find myself at that stage in my ministry having considerable sympathy with the laity and not finding it easy to assemble arguments to convince them of the necessity of bringing in an ordained person to preside. I have since become increasingly persuaded of the importance of an ordained person presiding at the Eucharist, though I am also convinced that the whole congregation are at the same time the celebrants – a communal meal in which all share and which all share in authenticating. The Roman Catholic theologian Schillebeeckx has interestingly argued that the people of God are entitled to have access to the sacrament of the Eucharist and so if no priest is available lay celebration should be allowed. Needless to say, his arguments did not carry weight with the Roman Catholic authorities.

Also during my time as Vicar of Holy Trinity, Margate, I encouraged the formation of Home groups for Bible Study and Fellowship. When I arrived as vicar there was just one group meeting and by the time I left there were over 20 groups. Often groups requested being able to share in Communion on occasion. Sometimes I or the curate would attend a group and preside at an informal Communion for them. On other occasions the leader of the group would lead an informal act of worship including the sharing of a meal which included taking bread and wine and sharing it as a group. However, I always argued that these occasions were not Anglican sacramental Communion services but could be viewed simply as Agape Fellowship meals.

I don't necessarily think that lockdown as a result of the Covid-19 Pandemic has brought about a growing consensus of eucharistic practice across theological divides but rather it has highlighted a trend that was already apparent across the different theological persuasions, namely an openness to learn from different theological traditions. In my Conservative Evangelical curacy days Anglo-Catholics and Liberals were viewed with great suspicion. During my incumbency at Holy Trinity, Margate, the three Anglican clergy in Margate and Cliftonville (a Charismatic neighbour, a Liberal Catholic and myself and my curate together with an Elim Pentecostal Pastor.) met regularly to pray together and through praying together found misconceptions and prejudices melted away as we discovered a common fellowship in Christ. Over the years as highlighted in earlier chapters my own experience, shared I believe by many others, has been a growing openness to traditions different from my own and a willingness to learn from those traditions. As a bishop appointing clergy to multi-parish benefices with a variety of theological outlooks in the different congregations,

I would ask potential candidates whether they would simply tolerate theological outlooks different from their own or would they be able not simply to accept different traditions but be willing to affirm them and learn from them.

Again as Bishop of Tewkesbury at various stages, I chaired the Council for WEMTC (West of England Theological Course). Where ordinands chose to train locally on WEMTC rather than attending a theological college in their own tradition (many Evangelical ordinands chose to attend Trinity College, Bristol, or Wycliffe Hall in a clear Evangelical tradition and ethos) they emerged at the end of training (with a few exceptions) much more open to respect and learn from theological traditions and practices different from their own. I regarded this as a positive advantage of training on a course alongside other ordinands of a different theological outlook.

In the *Church Times* for 21 January, 2022, there was a review of a book by Richard Burridge: *Holy Communion in Contagious Times: Celebrating in the Everyday and Online Worlds*. Richard argues that a Eucharist celebrated on a webinar platform such as Zoom "which allows us to be present to one another and to the Triune God at the same chronological moment in time ... and the same digital and physical space" satisfies all the criteria for Holy Communion. Referring to a woman, he writes:

> I cannot understand why her bread and wine which I can see and touch and pray over on my lap-top screen, cannot be open to the real presence of Christ as much as my own bread and wine ... As celebrant I intend to be a channel whereby God can bless her with his grace in bread and wine similarly; it is her intention and heartfelt desire as a lay person to feed on him with thanksgiving.

He goes on to ask: "Are these not valid and effective sacramental intentions? And if not, why not?" Richard specifically argues against the guidance put out by the National Church of England Communications team:

> Participants in a streamed service of Holy Communion should not be encouraged to place bread and wine before their screens. Joining together to share in the one bread and the one cup as those physically present to one another is integral to the service of Holy Communion; this is not possible under the current restrictions and it is not helpful to suggest otherwise. Any idea of remote consecration of the bread and wine should be avoided.

I confess that I find Richard Burridge's arguments convincing. If we believe in a God who is present everywhere by his Spirit why can he not take the bread and wine offered in a person's home in the context of an online service in which we are spiritually one though physically absent from one another and feed the recipient spiritually with the presence of the living, omni-present Christ. However, the House of Bishops has not been persuaded by Richard's arguments.

Chapter 9

The Local Parish Church Central to Church of England Ecclesiology

I mentioned in my opening chapter that the parish system has a very long-standing history traced back to being introduced in the seventh century by Theodore the Archbishop of Canterbury. This marks the ministry of Church of England clergy as distinct from their Roman Catholic or Free Church colleagues. It gives them spiritual responsibility for every man, woman and child in the parish whether or not they are churchgoers. In many more traditional parts of the country the local vicar will still receive a warm welcome if he or she appears on the doorstep of any of their parishioners. The local vicar is still likely to be the first port of call if a parishioner is looking for spiritual or pastoral support. The so-called Occasional Offices of baptisms, marriages and funerals though less called on than 25 or 50 years ago still provide an evangelistic opportunity for the local vicar. When a new vicar is installed in a parish or group of parishes in addition to welcomes from Church members, it is usual for the new priest to be welcomed by members of the wider community including non-church members.

Many of my Evangelical friends have worked with a "gathered" Church outlook that in my view is more of a Free Church ecclesiology rather than a distinctive Anglican ecclesiology. In my curacy days Emmanuel, Northwood, was a "gathered" church of like-minded Evangelicals; it drew in people from as much as a ten-mile radius who chose to attend because of its clear biblical teaching and excellent ministry with children and young people.

A Cambridge College Chapel Serving as a "Parish Church"

At Cambridge many of my Evangelical friends ignored College Chapel and chose on a Sunday to attend one of the Evangelical Churches in Cambridge, either the Round Church or Holy Trinity where Charles Simeon had been a leading Evangelical clergyman at the time of the Evangelical Revival. At Corpus Christi College, Cambridge, there was less suspicion of College Chapel among CICCU members. We were privileged to have John Bowker as our Chaplain. During his time as a student at Oxford he had belonged to OICCU and though he had later parted company over their view of the infallibility of Scripture, he maintained warm relationships with all of us as members of CICCU in Corpus. During my four years at Corpus, I found myself nurtured spiritually both by the specifically Evangelical life of CICCU and at the same time by the Anglican ethos of the College Chapel with its Anglican liturgy and its strong choral tradition.

Though only a small percentage of undergraduates attended Chapel, it played a significant role in the life of the College very much along the lines of a parish church in a parish setting. This was brought home to me very powerfully at the time of a tragedy in the life of the college. One of my fellow undergraduates was the son of the then Dean of Worcester. Tragically, unknown to any of us before coming to Corpus he had suffered from bouts of manic depression. On a particular weekend his girlfriend had been up for the weekend. He had seen her back on the train at Oxford Station on an early Sunday evening and appeared to be in excellent high spirits. He had then returned to his room and gassed himself. In those days sadly that was still possible. In a small college with only 180 undergraduates the whole college community was shell-shocked. It was hard to understand how in a close-knit small community someone could take their own life without others in the community being aware of the danger of that happening.

John Bowker laid on a special service in the College Chapel which was attended by the vast majority of students, many of whom would not normally have graced the chapel with their presence. I still remember 60 years later John Bowker early on in the service reading from Psalm 130: "Out of the depths I have cried unto Thee, O Lord." I cannot remember what he said in his address, but I do recall that it was incredibly appropriate and helpful to a community grieving for the loss of one of its number and feeling guilty that somehow we had failed this individual. In that situation John Bowker functioned very much as a parish priest functions in being available to parishioners in times of joy and in times of personal sadness and personal tragedy.

Gloucester Diocese and the Place of the Parish Church at the Heart of the Community

Both during my time as archdeacon in Guildford diocese and as Suffragan Bishop in Gloucester diocese I was aware of parish priests being the focus for helping people in the community, whether church attenders or not, coming to terms with a tragedy involving a member of the community. In Thornbury in Gloucester diocese a teenager was tragically killed and the parish priest opened the church to become a focus for young people's grief and to offer a message of Christian comfort and hope. In a parish on the edge of Guildford during my time as archdeacon a woman was murdered and again the parish priest was able to bring the community together enabling people to express their grief and shock. For me the privilege of being a key person in the community at such times is very much tied in with a historic Anglican understanding of parish ministry.

The Part Played by the Parish Church in My Own Upbringing

The Church of England focus on the parish played a significant part in my own engagement with the church as I grew up. Because the Church of England was the State Church and because in the 1950s most people still viewed themselves as Christians, the parish church was the natural place to attend if someone didn't have a clear allegiance to another denomination. So though my father and his family took an interest in the Theosophy movement and my father was more interested in Eastern religion (he kept a copy of the Hindu Upanishads by his bed which he read every night), my mother had been christened by her parents and though she had not been a regular churchgoer, she used to pray with me last thing at night and from an early age sent me to Sunday School at the local church and enrolled me from the age of 7 in the Church choir. So thanks to the place of the parish church in the local community I was introduced from an early age to the life of the local church in a Liberal Catholic tradition. At that stage that was the only tradition I was aware of though I did occasionally attend a Deanery celebration of the Guild of the Servants of the Sanctuary which was more distinctively Anglo-Catholic. At that stage I had no experience of the Evangelical tradition and I have no recollection of meeting any Christians who would have seen themselves as Evangelical.

Interestingly, there was a couple who took an interest in me as a teenager who were intimately involved with Moral Re-armament (MRA). MRA was founded in 1938 by Frank Buchman, an American Minister. I suspect looking back that they may have been of an Evangelical persuasion but the main influence they sought to exercise over me was moral rather than spiritual.

Wycliffe College Missions and the Parish

At different stages in my ministry I found myself appreciating the place of the parish in Anglican ecclesiology. During my six years as Vice-Principal of Wycliffe Hall, I was privileged to be involved with College Missions. Each Easter vacation students were expected to sign up for one of several college missions led by college tutors to a variety of parish settings round the country. On two occasions I was involved in leading a group of very gifted students to Norbury Parish Church in Hazel Grove in Chester diocese. Usually, we didn't take a team to the same parish on a second occasion, but on this occasion we had been invited to go back three years later and it was encouraging to witness spiritual fruit from the first mission and to be privileged to witness quite a spiritual movement during the second mission. One of our students, Paul Brice, was extremely gifted in multimedia presentations and he organised with other students a series of evening meetings on the nature of the Church using a rich variety of media presentations.

The church had been through a dry patch but as a Church of England church it had been good at building links with the wider community (a distinctive opportunity for Church of England clergy and churches) and during the week of special presentations church members had been able to invite people from the wider community to come along to what were highly professional presentations. It was a reminder of the strength of the Church of England in making the most of the occasional offices, of baptisms, weddings and funerals, developing links though a church school and gaining entry into many areas of a parish because of its privileged position as the Established Church. I mentioned in an earlier chapter that we had some students at Wycliffe during my time who didn't set great store by this distinctive Anglican ethos and were more inclined to adopt a Free Church Ecclesiology, sitting light to the parish system, the life of the deanery and diocesan life operating with a model of an independent church drawing in like-minded people from a wide area rather than seeking to engage in a serious way with those living in the parish.

Students also had parish placements during their training and staff members were encouraged to go and see them leading services and preaching in these placements. Many of the parish placements were in rural contexts. Spending time with students in these settings, I came to have a deep appreciation of the value of the village church at the heart of the village community. Many village congregations struggled on a weekly basis but on a number of occasions in the year (Christmas, Mothering Sunday, Harvest, Remembrance Sunday and other special times) the village church could attract a large congregation. I remember one Christmas Eve visiting three village churches for "midnight Mass", one was as early as 8.00 p.m., one was at 10.00 p.m. and the third one was at 11.30 p.m. – it was quite a tour de force! But I recall being deeply impressed by the excellent attendance at each of these services. It would be easy to be critical of those attending because they might not be seen again in church for weeks or months and might have little or no understanding of discipleship (indeed, one honest man at the door greeted me at a Christmas service by saying "see you again on Easter Sunday!"). However, the presence of a church lovingly cared for and kept open by a small, committed congregation meant that people who might not otherwise have any meaningful contact with the Christian faith or experience of Christian worship were able on different occasions during the year to have such an encounter with the possibility of being drawn into a deeper faith. These opportunities would be lost if there ceased to be a church building at the heart of the village community.

A County-wide Event to Celebrate the New Millennium

Another aspect of the privilege of being the Established Church was brought home to me when I was Bishop of Tewkesbury.

During my time in Gloucester diocese along with the rest of the country (and indeed of the world), we marked the start of a new Millennium. At a gathering of Church Leaders in 1997 I asked the question whether we were planning to organise a celebration for Pentecost Sunday 2000 as was being suggested by the wider Churches Together in England group. I have learnt over the years that it can be unwise to ask such questions as you are likely to be given the task of organising the event! This happened to me on this occasion. I gathered together a group from the different denominations. I chaired the overall planning group but set up a number of other groups to organise different aspects of the day. I approached Edward Gillespie who ran the racecourse (he is a practising Christian) and he wonderfully agreed to make the racecourse available to us virtually free of charge, just a small amount to cover the cost of hiring people to clean the site at the end of the day. Later, the Greenbelt Festival was to move onto Cheltenham Racecourse for a number of years and our special celebration on Pentecost Saturday, 2000, was very much like a Greenbelt Festival fitted into a single day. There were masses of stalls, seminars, events for children, music groups playing on the big stage, and we ended the day with a spectacular firework display for which I managed to secure special funding. Again, through being the Established Church we were able to have Princess Anne join us on the day and spend an hour walking round the site – she was brilliant. We obtained a lottery fund grant of £25,000. I was especially pleased to be introduced by one of our parish priests (now himself a bishop) to the husband of one of his church members in a multi-parish benefice who was Managing Director of a local company. In addition to him giving us a gift of £40,000 from his company's charitable funds, he told me over a breakfast meeting in a Cheltenham hotel (he was so busy he chose to have early meetings with me over breakfast!) that the event provided a great training opportunity for his media staff. So they provided us with outstanding professional media coverage at the same time as paying us for the privilege of providing an event that was ideal for training them in media coverage. Fifteen thousand people turned up on the day (our prayers for fine weather were answered) and it was a great success and a great opportunity for ecumenical cooperation and drawing on the rich variety of lay gifts in the various activities of the day. I believe it was possible to lay on such an event because the Church was seen as not only at the heart of the local parish but also at the heart of the county.

Because of the privileged position of the Church of England as the State Church it is possible for bishops to take initiatives to highlight important issues. Bishop Olivia, the Bishop of Reading in Oxford diocese, is one of three bishops who lead the Church of England work on the Environment. On Friday 21 April, 2023, she was joined by thousands of others, different charities and faith organisations, in supporting "The Big One" Climate protest in Westminster, and as a bishop she invited others from Oxford diocese and farther afield to join with her.

Parish-based Ministry in Semi-Retirement as a House for Duty Priest

As a bishop I knew I needed to retire at the age of 70. My diocesan bishop was quite keen to be able to appoint my successor before he himself retired. Also, the demands of episcopal ministry as I approached my late 60s began to feel quite burdensome. Many of my university friends in their 50s had retired from full-time work but carried on with consultancy on a part-time basis reducing over several years to a four-day week and then a three-day week and eventually to just one day a week. I was aware that suddenly to stop working would be a shock to the system. Also, my wife and I had been slightly slow getting into the housing market ready for retirement so to be provided with housing for a few more years while being in a less pressured job was attractive. My wife had always fully shared in ministry with me and we felt that as we had started out together in parish based ministry it would be attractive to end our ministry together in a parish.

In Gloucester diocese with its 400 churches, we had increasingly found it helpful to create House for Duty posts in parishes with a smaller population, so I was familiar with House for Duty ministry. House for Duty ministry offers a retired priest a house free of charge in return for Sunday plus two days a week ministry. Dioceses vary in the terms; in Gloucester we allowed House for Duty clergy to retain a proportion of the fee for any weddings or funerals they officiated at. Oxford diocese, where I ended up serving, did not allow me to keep a portion of the fee for weddings and funerals. This was a shame as I ended up developing an extensive weddings ministry but more of that later. As I approached retirement in 2013, I wrote to a number of bishops indicating that I would be interested in a House for Duty post. I saw an advertisement in the *Church Times* for a House for Duty post in the Chenies benefice in Oxford diocese with special responsibility for Latimer and Flaunden, two small villages. I duly applied and was short-listed.

On the interview day I discovered that the other short-listed candidate for the post was already settled in the benefice working as children and family worker paid for by the benefice and was an OLM priest having undergone ordination training and been ordained while working with children and families in the benefice. As we drove home at the end of the day, I commented to my wife that I felt it was not a foregone conclusion that I would be offered the post and also asked how we would feel if the post was offered and it meant the local OLM wasn't appointed. We learnt later that the Flaunden parish representatives wanted the person they already knew and loved and were suspicious that a retired bishop would regard it as beneath him to get involved in the nitty-gritty of parish life! The Latimer parish representatives, however, were adamant that they wanted me. A wise archdeacon broke through the deadlock by suggesting that both of us were appointed. She argued that as a bishop I would be likely to pick up some wider responsibilities in the deanery and diocese and so it could be helpful for me to focus largely just on Latimer leaving the local candidate to focus especially on Flaunden though with both of us playing a part in the wider benefice. So just after Easter, 2013, we moved into the rectory in Latimer and embarked on House for Duty ministry.

I have mentioned before that one of the differences between a Free Church minister and a Church of England vicar is that the Free Church minister serves a congregation drawn potentially from a wide area, while a vicar serves everyone living in the parish whether or not they attend church services. This gives a vicar grounds for reaching out to all of his or her parishioners. As a bishop I had often heard complaints from parishioners that their parish priest no longer believed in visiting. Because the population of the village was not large, I decided early on that I would aim to visit every home in the parish in the course of my first year. Every afternoon I set out to visit systematically. Inevitably people weren't always in. I would leave a card to indicate I had visited. However, many people were at home, a mix of non-working wives, retired people and men and women working from home. With only a few exceptions I was usually invited in, offered the proverbial cuppa and people were very happy for me to pray for them before leaving. I suspect it helped being a bishop, though the fact that I was visiting on behalf of the Church of the Nation undoubtedly also opened doors.

When I was bishop, one of the clergy in the Forest of Dean had been particularly successful in building up a sizeable congregation. He had shared with me part of his secret. Whenever there was a special service, he would text people he had had a link with extending an invitation to them to attend the special service. I was not into texting but as I visited door to door, I asked those I was visiting whether they were happy to give me their email address. No one refused so I quickly built up a list of people's email addresses which enabled me to keep in touch with them. I would extend a personal invitation to our monthly All Age Service and to special occasions such as Carols by Candlelight and other special Christmas services including a Nine Lessons and Carols which I re-introduced, Mothering Sunday, Easter, Harvest, Remembrance. The personal approach paid dividends and we ended up with very good congregations on those special occasions.

Parish Ministry and the Occasional Offices

Another distinctiveness about parish ministry as a Church of England priest is the opportunities provided by the Occasional Offices of Baptisms, Weddings and Funerals. When I was Vicar of Holy Trinity, Margate, the curate and I introduced a "closed" policy to baptisms. This was partly in reaction to a very open policy at Emmanuel, Northwood, where I served my curacy and being aware that over my time there an open, welcoming policy had not resulted in a single family who requested baptism for their children being brought into the worship life of the church. Our policy in Margate (it was not very hard-line but we insisted that couples attended a few services before agreeing a date for the baptism and insisted on preparation with the couple) had resulted in a significant number of couples discovering a Christian faith and becoming regular members of the congregation, though there were others who were alienated and as a neighbouring parish priest frustratingly was happy to offer afternoon baptism to anyone, he did pick up some of our parishioners who weren't happy with our policy. Though I was generally happy with the closed policy we operated, over time I became increasingly concerned that with the single-parent families living on the Council Estate opposite the Church there was a risk that our approach represented yet another rejection in their lives (my curate I think didn't share my concerns). Interestingly, my successor at Holy Trinity (who later went on to be Bishop of Dorchester in Oxford diocese) changed over to a more open policy and saw a number of couples come to faith through his more open policy.

When I moved to Latimer as House for Duty priest, some 40 years had passed since I was vicar in Margate and the place of the Church in the wider community had undoubtedly changed significantly. In the 1970s the vicar was still viewed as a person of some significance in the community. By 2013 that privileged sense of status had largely disappeared. Far fewer people were active church-attenders. More people had had a negative experience of Church and often found it unwelcoming. So I felt that I needed to present a face of a village church that was open and welcoming. We didn't have a great number of baptisms but those that we did have by offering a warm welcome resulted in families attending at least our monthly All Age Service and in some cases attending more regularly. We also started up a monthly Messy Church in the Parish Room next to the church. It never resulted in great numbers but did enable us to engage with several families who didn't attend main Sunday services. My dear late wife was a very significant person in organising and leading Messy Church together with a lay member of the congregation.

Weddings Ministry

The Church in Latimer stood in the grounds of what originally had been the Stately Home of the Lord Cheshams. During the Second World War the house was taken over by the Government and when the war ended the combined Forces took over the house for training Officers. Later on, it became a hotel and was a weddings venue. My immediate predecessor hadn't shown any interest in developing a weddings ministry. I saw the presence of a weddings venue hotel right by the village church as a gift. I arranged early on to meet up with the hotel Weddings coordinator and encouraged her to ask wedding couples whether they would like a church wedding. Most couples assumed that they couldn't have a church wedding if they didn't live in the village or if one of them had been divorced. I suggested to her that it would be helpful to encourage couples to have a conversation with me as it might be possible for them to have a church wedding. As a result of my overtures to the hotel we were able to develop a weddings ministry which in my final year saw me officiating at over 20 weddings. The hotel began to advertise the presence of a church in the grounds of the hotel as a selling point as a Weddings venue. It was good news for the hotel and good news for a village church with only a small regular congregation and good news financially for the church! I explained to couples who didn't live in the village or have a historical link with the village that they would have to attend services for six months before the wedding and I found that they were more than happy to attend. I didn't insist on them coming every Sunday, but to attend at least once a month. Many continued to come to church after the wedding and towards the end of my time, I had the privilege of baptising some babies of couples I had married earlier in my ministry. Those who were divorced had to have a conversation about the circumstances of their divorce and again I found couples were happy to have those conversations. Marriage preparation was offered at benefice level and those marriage preparation days became very popular with the young couples as they greatly enjoyed meeting other young couples preparing to get married. One of the preparation days was on a Sunday with a special service for the couples followed by a meal kindly provided by the hotel for us all and then a time to explore practical questions relating to their weddings. For one of these preparation occasions, I managed to get the Revd Dr Sandra Millar who at the time headed up the Church of England outreach through the Occasional Offices to preach at the service and engage with the couples over lunch and answer their various questions. She was encouraged to see a village church making the most of the opportunities provided by one of the significant life events.

The Church at the Heart of Village Life

An atheist parishioner whom I got to know paid me a lovely compliment after I had been in the parish for a year. He commented that I had helped foster a strong sense of community whether or not people attended Sunday worship. We organised a number of celebration events, for example, for the Queen's Jubilee, which involved the whole community. I became aware early on of a division between the older traditional part of the village and Parkfield where the Forces personnel had been housed. Those living in what they saw as the "proper" village resented the "newcomers" who had taken up residence in Parkfield when the Forces personnel moved out. The village church was the only place where people from both halves of the village met. The Queen's Jubilee was an interesting example of that division. I discovered early on that the "Village" was planning its own celebration and that Parkfield was planning a separate celebration. I had to work hard but managed to persuade both parties that to have two separate celebrations in such a small community was really rather absurd and we were able to bring both parties together for a joint celebration based round the church and hotel. Being a priest in the Established Church undoubtedly made it easier to be viewed as someone at the heart of a traditional village community, held in respect by the majority and able to exercise a leadership role in community events.

Another offshoot of being the Established Church at the heart of the community enabled my wife to write a history of Staverton the farming village we lived in on the edge of Cheltenham when I was Bishop of Tewkesbury and then also to write a history of

Latimer village. Both involved a lot of hard work and research but were very widely appreciated. The history of Latimer which she produced with a local printer including colour photos was launched with a special community event. Everyone in the village (with only a handful of exceptions) purchased a copy, the Hotel kept copies at Reception which were often bought by people staying in the hotel with an interest in the village. After covering her costs, she raised quite a sizeable amount of money for the church.

The genius of the Church of England historically has been for the church to be at the heart of the community. As people in the wake of the industrial revolution moved out of the countryside into towns and cities it was harder for the church to continue to be at the heart of very large communities or for a vicar to be known personally by all of his or her parishioners. However, in rural areas I believe it is still possible for the church to be at the heart of the community and for community events to revolve around the church and I was privileged to see that being worked out very effectively during my six years' ministry as a House for Duty priest in Latimer.

National Debate in the Church of England About the Place of the Local Parish Church

When I was bishop as a Bishop's Staff in Gloucester diocese, we were only too well aware that with reducing numbers of full-time stipendiary clergy it wasn't easy to maintain ministry across the 400 churches, many of them serving small communities with very small congregations. However, we were very reluctant to close village churches. We recognised that as Methodist churches struggled to survive, the Methodist leadership chose to close churches believing that the remaining members would move to the nearest Methodist church in a nearby town. However, that didn't happen; members either chose to attend the village Church of England church or simply stopped going to church and so the result was a further weakening of the Methodist Church nationally. I confess that I don't have hard evidence for this; it was rather an impression gained from talking to Anglicans and Methodists in the villages of Gloucester diocese during my 17 years as Bishop of Tewkesbury.

In *The Telegraph* for Saturday 5 June, 2021, there was an article by Emma Thompson with the title "Out of touch bishops are pushing the Church to the brink of ruin". Earlier in the week there was a news item about the Bishop of Winchester standing down for a period of time because there was the threat of a "no confidence in his leadership" motion being tabled at Diocesan Synod by a number of leading clergy and lay people in the diocese. He has since taken early retirement. Emma talked about the Bishop of Winchester proposing to cut clergy numbers and merge village churches. She referred to the vicar of a friend of hers who had got up at 3.00 a.m. to bless a dying baby; this vicar was due to retire in 2022 and was unlikely to be replaced. Emma went on to argue that rural dwellers love their parish church. She went on to comment that the attachment to the local is seen as a problem by the Church of England "hierarchy" whereas in her view it should be seen as part of the solution. My experience as a suffragan bishop in a diocese that included many Cotswold village churches and then as House for Duty priest in a Buckinghamshire village very much confirmed the view that parishioners are much more likely to attend a church local to where they live. We might long for them to show signs of a deeper discipleship that would be prepared to get into a car and drive a few miles to a large church centre, but the reality is that the vast majority of them would not entertain the possibility of doing so.

In *The Daily Telegraph* for Tuesday 4 January, 2022, there was an article with the heading "Shocking threat to parishes as more than 400 churches close in less than a decade". It claimed that senior clergy warned of the shocking threat to parishes as "the bedrock of the Church of England". It argued that analysis of the Church of England data revealed that 423 churches were closed between 2010 and 2019. Further analysis, it claimed, revealed that 940 churches were closed between 1987 and 2019. The author of the article went on to write, "I share the concern of many people that the policies that lead to the closure of churches may also mean that we will be seeing more and more changes to the parish system which is, after all, the bedrock of the life of the Church of England for England." As mentioned already, the parish system can be traced back to the seventh century introduced by the then Archbishop of Canterbury, Theodore of Tarsus; so it has a very long and respectable history. It has been a distinctive characteristic of the Church in England for some 1400 years. However, as also mentioned above, social and cultural changes since the Industrial Revolution and changes in more recent times in the wake of a technological revolution to patterns of social relationships do raise questions about the relevance of parish based ministry in the twenty-first century.

Not very far away from Latimer village where I served as House for Duty priest was a church plant known as Latimer Minster headed up by Frog Orr-Ewing. Frog was recognised as a Church of England minister authorised by the late Bishop of Buckingham an area bishop in the Diocese of Oxford. Latimer Minster is not a parish church but operates alongside the parishes of the Buckingham area within Oxford diocese. At a Deanery Chapter meeting held on the site of Latimer Minster, I was chatting to some of the lay members of the Minster and was interested to discover that they travelled all the way from High Wycombe (probably over 20 miles away) and all of them had been drawn into the life of the Minster through friendship with Christians living in High Wycombe and worshipping at the Minster. So the life and growth of the church grew through relationships formed across a very wide geographical area rather than being drawn into the life of one's local parish church. This seems to be the way that many church plants in a Charismatic-Evangelical tradition grow rather than through the traditional parish system: associational rather than a community model.

If I were an Evangelical with a Free Church outlook, I would probably be very happy to see parish churches closed in rural areas and focus on ensuring that there were large well-supported churches in main centres of population to which people could travel and enjoy belonging to an associational model of church. However, as an Evangelical committed to also being a good Anglican, I believe in ensuring the continuity of parish churches even in rural areas with a small population. I believe that there is a place for a parish church at the heart of a community and recent correspondence in the Church Press and in national Newspapers would suggest that that view is shared by a significant number of people many of whom are not weekly churchgoers but do want a church at the heart of their community which they can attend on special occasions.

Changing Patterns of Ministry but Retaining Churches at the Heart of Village Life

However, it is also clear that the way ministry is managed across the different dioceses has to change. When I was Bishop of Tewkesbury, my wife and I lived in Staverton a traditional farming village on the edge of Cheltenham. We lived in what had been the vicarage for Staverton which had had its own full-time vicar earlier in the twentieth century. By the time we were living there Staverton was part of a benefice that included seven parishes. At the beginning of the twentieth century there were approximately 27,000 full-time parochial clergy. The official figure for 2019 was 7700 stipendiary clergy. At the beginning of the twentieth century all the clergy were full-time stipendiary and male. However, in the course of the next 100 years or so patterns of ordained ministry had changed considerably. So in 2019 in addition to the 7700 stipendiary clergy there were 2870 self-supporting clergy, 1020 ordained chaplains, 1010 clergy in other posts, 7370 clergy with Permission to Officiate (PTO), most of them retired clergy. I often reflected while Bishop of Tewkesbury that we couldn't have sustained ministry in the Diocese of Gloucester without our retired clergy. The other significant change of course was the passing of legislation to allow women to be ordained as priests. Just under a third of all clergy in 2019 were women and of those ordained in 2019, 51% were women. Another significant statistic in 2019 was that there were 7830 Licensed Lay Readers (referred to in some dioceses as Licensed Lay Ministers), many of them involved regularly in preaching and in leading non-eucharistic services.

With significantly fewer full-time stipendiary clergy it doesn't require a lot of imagination to recognise that the way parish ministry is provided has to be significantly different from the time when there were over three times as many stipendiary clergy. Another significant factor that made a difference during the twentieth century was a rediscovery of the ministry of the whole people of God. This was in part as a result of the Charismatic Movement with its focus on the Holy Spirit equipping lay people to discover and exercise God-given gifts, though the Charismatic movement wasn't the only factor; there was a wider movement encouraging lay people to discover and exercise their gifts as represented in the book *God's Frozen People* by Mark Gibbs and Ralph T Morton about the importance of lay ministry. A significant focus of David Bentley's ministry as Bishop of Gloucester during my time as his suffragan bishop was the development of lay ministry teams. The focus of these teams was definitely not about helping over-stretched and over-worked clergy but rather about recapturing the New Testament model reflected in 1 Corinthians 12, Romans 12, 1 Peter 2 and 4 and especially Ephesians 4 of ministry belonging to the whole people of God and the role of the clergy being to facilitate and equip lay people to discover and exercise their God-given gifts.

In some of the multi-parish benefices this led to a rich flowering of lay gifts and often as lay people discovered their gifts and their distinctive ministries some felt a calling to ordained ministry. Ordained Local Ministers emerged from these teams. Historically with stipendiary clergy the call to ordained ministry was seen as originating in an individual having a personal sense of call which was then tested initially in the local diocese and then by a national discernment process. The focus of Ordained Local Ministry was different. It was about a local community identifying one or more of its lay people and saying to them, we believe you have the gifts that are needed in this church and so we invite you to give serious consideration to the possibility of being ordained to serve our local community. The vocation rather than being a very personal individualistic vocation was seen as emerging from the local congregation reflecting on the challenges and opportunities for ministry and mission in the local context and then identifying those the local congregation believed had the gifts to facilitate that ministry and mission.

Certainly, Local Ministry Teams had a mixed history but there were places where they flourished and resulted in a renewed sense of ministry and mission. Some clergy sadly felt threatened when very able lay people emerged with significant gifts and as a result felt de-skilled. When Michael Perham followed David Bentley as Bishop of Gloucester, he put much more emphasis on the central importance of the ordained clergy and the result was that many of the lay ministry teams felt sidelined and undervalued and as a result didn't flourish in the same way during Bishop Michael's time as bishop.

In 1983 John Tiller was Director of Ministry in the Church of England and produced a report for the Ministry Division of the Church of England: *A Strategy for the Church's Ministry*. By the early 1980s the Church of England was aware of a considerable reduction in the number of stipendiary priests and was predicting an even greater reduction in the following years. The Tiller Report majored on focusing on priests with two different callings and a different focus for their ministry. There would be diocesan priests equipped to exercise strategic oversight across a deanery and locally ordained priests (self-supporting) entrusted with the pastoral care of local congregations. At the time the Report was viewed very negatively, but during my time as Bishop of Tewkesbury the archdeacons and myself often commented that in the rapidly changing situation of the Church of England the Tiller Report made a lot of sense.

In *The Daily Telegraph* for Monday 10 January, 2022, there was an article with the heading "Sunday Church numbers have halved in the past 30 years". There is a suggestion that priests covering more than one parish has sparked a "loss of confidence" in the Church. The article drew attention to the fact that the only diocese to buck the trend was London diocese which has stuck to the one priest, one parish model. London diocese has seen a slight increase in church attendance during the same period when the overall number of Sunday worshippers nationally fell by about 40%. However, London being an entirely urban context cannot easily be compared to rural dioceses and there are likely to be a number of factors responsible for London seeing growth when other dioceses saw decline. The article quotes the Revd Marcus Walker, founder of the Save the Parish campaign who argues that "we need theologically trained priests embedded in their communities with the time to know and love the people they serve". However, there is a pragmatic issue of where such priests in sufficient number are going to be found and if it is an unrealistic vision then maybe other possibilities, however unpopular, may have to be explored.

Towards the end of 2021 bishops were in the news with reference to a vision document coming before General Synod encouraging the identifying of 10,000 lay leaders to engage in church planting. The vision came from the New Wine Conference on Church Planting. It has to be acknowledged that many New Wine Churches operate on a Free Church model of the Church, an Associational model drawing on like-minded people from a wide geographical area rather than a traditional parish model. The vision document has stirred up some very angry responses from those committed to the Church of England's historical parish system and people fear there is a hidden agenda to do away with the traditional parish system. Both archbishops have sought to reassure people that there is no hidden agenda and rather than these new church plants replacing parish churches, it is a question of a mixed economy church, a both/and church, church plants existing alongside parish churches.

I have referred earlier in this chapter to Latimer Minister headed up by Frog Orr-Ewing and his wife, Amy. It was set up in 2010 and given permission by the late Bishop of Buckingham for this non-parochial church plant. The model of church is associational rather than the traditional Anglican parochial model. Their website speaks of the church having a passionate desire to be a greater resource to the wider church in the nation and beyond by reaching, raising and releasing this generation locally, regionally and across the world! No small vision! Gerrards Cross which is next door to where Latimer Minister is situated is a very lively Evangelical-Charismatic church and certainly many of the clergy in the Amersham deanery where Frog and Amy were allowed to plant their Fresh Expression of Church were not very happy about it and wondered why they chose to plant in an area already very well resourced in terms of church life. In addition to Gerrards Cross Anglican Church, there is Gold Hill Baptist Church in the area (an extremely large and vibrant church) and also another lively Anglican Evangelical Church in Chalfont St Peter, all very close by. The local clergy thought they would have done better to explore planting a church plant in a tough area of the diocese where churches might be struggling.

As I settled into ministry in Latimer, I was aware of quite a number of committed Christians who every Sunday got into their cars to travel to churches farther afield, some to Christ Church, Chorleywood, quite a number to Gold Hill Baptist Church in Chalfont St Peter. If just some of them had been prepared to support their local village church it could have opened up much greater opportunities for ministry and mission. However, I do understand that if you are Christian parents with young children or teenagers you want for their sake to be part of a church that has the resources to provide lively children's and youth ministry and a village church isn't in a position to do that.

So I do recognise the place for Fresh Expressions of Church alongside traditional parish churches in the hope that people who are not reached by their local parish church may be reached through friendships by lively Fresh Expressions. As St Paul writes in his first letter to the Corinthians "by all means to reach some". Rowan Williams when he was Archbishop of Canterbury helpfully spoke of a mixed economy, Fresh Expressions of Church alongside traditional expressions of Church and many others have rightly picked up on the importance of the mixed economy, appropriate for a church that manages to contain within it many different theological traditions and outlooks, unity in diversity, reflecting the Trinitarian life of God.

Chapter 10

Reflections on the Impact of Covid Lockdown on Our Understanding and Practice of Church

Lockdown as a result of the pandemic has had some significant impact both on the way we understand Church and the way we practise Church. Questions have been raised about the importance of sacred space, about the need to meet physically together, about the sacrament of the Eucharist, about being committed to a local church. In addition, the negative financial impact of the pandemic on church life has raised questions about how viable small congregations in rural areas and inner-city areas are and will they be able to survive and that in turn raises questions about the continuing importance of the local parish church serving its local community.

The Importance of Sacred Space

I have reflected at some length in a previous chapter about how as a result of time spent at Tantur in the Holy Land, I came to appreciate for the first time in my Christian life the importance of sacred space. As a result of time spent in the Holy Land, I began to be involved in leading Pilgrimages to the Holy Land. I served on the Council of the Bible Reading Fellowship (BRF) for many years chairing the Executive Committee and initially Richard Fisher, the Chief Executive of BRF, and I led pilgrimages together as an extension of the ministry of BRF in encouraging Christians to engage with Scripture and aware that the Holy Land is often described as "the Fifth Gospel". Later on, my wife and I led Pilgrimages together and it was a joy to observe what an enormous spiritual impact spending time in the places where Jesus lived and ministered had on each group of pilgrims. When you lead pilgrimages, you tend to attract over time people who appreciate your distinctive style of leadership and they become "groupies"! As a result those who became regular supporters requested us to take them to other places on Pilgrimage and we were privileged to lead a group to Jordan and Syria when it was safe to go to Syria, also in the Footsteps of St Paul taking in places in Greece and also Ephesus, Rhodes and Crete and also a pilgrimage embracing the Seven Churches of Asia Minor as addressed by the Risen Christ in Revelation chapters 2 and 3.

Being unable to meet in church during lockdown as a result of the pandemic and meeting virtually online threw up an interesting range of questions for Christians of different theological persuasions. As mentioned in an earlier chapter, my wife and I in retirement have chosen to be linked with a church that would describe itself as in the Liberal Catholic tradition. It is a multi-cultural congregation embracing people from the West Indies, India, Pakistan, Sri Lanka, Hong Kong and other parts of the world. Inevitably, in such a culturally mixed congregation there are significantly different theological outlooks. The vicar helpfully holds together in a very Anglican way both a focus on good biblical preaching and a focus on the central importance of the Eucharist. During lockdown we began to meet online, many of us sharing in a service streamed on Zoom and also made available on Facebook. Our vicar was not happy celebrating the Eucharist on her own and not happy with the practice of encouraging some people in their own homes to set aside bread and wine and communicate in that way, so as a result all of our online services with the exception of Christmas and Easter were non-eucharistic with an emphasis on spiritual encounter with the risen Christ through Scripture and Prayer.

Has the experience of online worship during the pandemic raised questions about the need for specially dedicated, consecrated buildings for Christians to meet in? When I was Bishop of Tewkesbury, I would quite often when talking with

Church members remind them that though the 400 church buildings in the diocese, many of them Grade 1 listed, were a reminder of the presence of Christian faith at the heart of rural and urban communities, every single church building could be destroyed, but the Church of Jesus Christ would still survive in the lives of his disciples.

I have already referred to Justin Welby as Archbishop of Canterbury presiding on Easter Morning at a Eucharist from his kitchen table. Quite a number of Christians felt that was not an appropriate setting for a celebration of a solemn sacrament.

Is It Important to Belong to a Local Church?

During lockdown many Christians went online to share in the worship of well-known vibrant churches. The internet makes it possible for someone sitting in the comfort of their own home to join with Christians in their worship anywhere not only in this country but anywhere in the world. In many cases such worship would be much livelier and more enriching than what was experienced in one's local church. So when lockdown ended was there a temptation not to return Sunday by Sunday to one's local church?

Undoubtedly also during lockdown some churchgoers got out of the habit of sharing in worship on a weekly basis. It is the experience of very many churches that average Sunday attendance post-lockdown is significantly lower than before the pandemic.

Are Rural Churches More at Risk as a Result of the Pandemic?

Leslie Francis and Andrew Village conducted a survey during lockdown on the impact of the pandemic on fragile rural churches. They drew on the work of Anne Lawson and her series of three papers published in *Rural Theology*. Anne conducted interviews and organised focus groups among rural clergy serving multiple parishes. She identified five particular burdens for such clergy: administration, presence in multiple places, isolation, distance, visibility. In addition, she identified five marks of fragile rural churches that brought anxiety to clergy serving those parishes: financial pressures and anxiety about dwindling financial resources; inability to replace churchwardens and other lay officers; a lack of a critical mass of children and volunteers to work with young people; a lack of time to do new things and the relentless round of keeping the show on the road; tiny often single figure congregations. These marks could equally characterise clergy serving in inner city or tough urban parishes.

My own experience as Bishop of Tewkesbury in a diocese that included a large number of historic churches serving tiny congregations in the Cotswolds certainly supported evidence of diminishing congregations. Several of the Cotswold churches had single figure attendance on a normal Sunday. I recall on one occasion during a vacancy managing to cover all four services in one benefice in a Sunday morning; in one church I had a congregation of six, at another eight, another ten, at another twelve. I pointed out later to the key lay leaders that if they had combined for a united service, they would have had a congregation of 36 and would have been able to enjoy singing hymns rather than struggling to sing and a better sense of celebration, but, of course, no one was prepared to give up their service in their own much loved village church.

Reading the reflections of Anne Lawson and Leslie Francis and Andrew Village, I recognised significantly different kinds of experience of village church life. As Bishop of Tewkesbury, I used to describe village life in the Cotswolds as mini-suburban parishes as generally there was no shortage of money if a church, for example, needed a new roof or a new boiler. On one occasion when a Cotswold church needed major work undertaken, a church member got his cheque book out and wrote a cheque for

£10,000 to cover the cost. Though not common this experience would not have been totally unique. So the future of the church in some rural/village settings is not at risk on financial grounds, though might be in terms of attracting a critical mass of worshippers.

My experience in Gloucester diocese was that there was a reluctance to attend church anywhere other than one's own village church and I suspect that experience would be repeated in many other parts of the country. Hampnett was a hamlet (total population 330) very close to Northleach and part of a multi-parish benefice. A previous vicar pointed out that residents of Hampnett every Sunday drove to Northleach to get their Sunday paper but were totally opposed to the idea of driving to Northleach to attend a service. At a purely pragmatic level it would have made sense to close Hampnett church and encourage the congregation to join with Northleach. A previous vicar had suggested that and it went down like a lead balloon! Hampnett church is Norman dating back to 1125 with a fifteenth-century church tower. The chancel is almost entirely twelfth-century work. In 1871 the then vicar, Revd William Wiggin, had the chancel, the sanctuary and nave windows painted in a remarkably ornate pattern of mock-mediaeval stencilling. His parishioners were not impressed and tried to raise money to have the paintings removed or covered over with whitewash. Fortunately, they were unable to raise the necessary funds and so the church remains a unique example and attracts many visitors over the course of a year. As a bishop, I was able to understand why the parishioners were strongly opposed to any idea of closure.

Work has been undertaken by those involved with the Church Growth Movement that suggests that even in an age when people don't think twice about driving a distance for the weekly shop, for leisure pursuits and other reasons, they are more likely to attend church if there is a church within walking distance of where they live. Though usual Sunday attendance in many of the Cotswold village churches was often only just into double figures, for special occasions such as Christmas services, Mothering Sunday, Harvest, Remembrance and in some places also Easter, a very large percentage of the population would be present in their village church. As bishop, I had the privilege of presiding at special services in Cotswold churches and for special occasions a service could attract over 50% of the village population and on one famous occasion for a Christmas service we somehow managed to end up with a larger congregation than the entire population of the village!

Is the Future of the Parish Church Under Threat?

Again, I return to this topic which I have reflected on in a previous chapter. On the London Diocesan website posted 13 January, 2022, there is an interview with Revd H Miller, Associate Vicar at St Barnabas Kensington and "Creative Growth Ambition Lead for London Diocese". His role in other dioceses would probably be known as Mission Enabler. He has been in the diocese for about six years and has helped to lead the diocesan project to plant 100 new worshipping communities. He responds to a question about whether Church planting is an Anglican practice and whether we find it in Scripture and in Church history. He argues that every church was planted at some point in the past. He draws on evidence from the New Testament in support of planting new churches and in more recent Anglican history he refers to St Mary Abbots Church in Kensington in 1825 having made a commitment to plant two new congregations as it was a large parish. One congregation became St Barnabas, Kensington, and the other became Holy Trinity, Brompton! When I was Vicar of Holy Trinity, Margate, because the population of the parish increased considerably in my time as vicar with some substantial new estates being built on land that was previously agricultural land, I laid plans for planting a new church and under my successor a new church was built and eventually a new parish was formed of St Philip's, Palm Bay. In other models, characteristic of much Victorian Church history, it might have become a daughter church, but that model often hindered growth through being over dependent on the Mother church.

Miller refers to church planting across different church traditions. In the early nineteenth century there was a church planting movement in East London led by the Catholic wing of the Church of England.

People have expressed concern about church plants being lay led, but he argues that though there are lay leaders of new congregations they are always ultimately answerable to and under the authority of ordained clergy. He gives an example of **The Grove** which is a missional community planted on an estate in West London led by Mark Tate who isn't ordained but it comes under the authority of a local priest.

He argues that parishes so far from being sidelined are at the centre of church planting. The 2030 vision for London diocese includes the goal of planting 400 new worshipping communities and that number reflects the fact that there are approximately 400 existing parishes in the diocese, so the vision is for each parish to plant a new congregation. He affirms that the strength of the Church of England is that every square inch of the country is covered by a parish, and someone has the cure of souls of all who live there. He argues that it is out of the place of strength that it is possible to look at new ways to reach people.

The 2020 Vision for the Diocese of London saw the planting of 87 new worshipping communities in London and the vast majority of these were related to parish life and mission. Many of them were related to reaching specific language groups, so services were offered in Gujarati, Hindi, Turkish, Portuguese, Spanish, French, Italian and German, all of them born out of a desire to reach specific people groups who might not be reached by the traditional English speaking parish church.

There is a lot of talk in recent times in the Church of England of a mixed economy church and Miller uses the phrase of a mixed ecology as essential to the well-being of the church. He argues that a strong parish system is vital for the health of the Church of England, but that there is also a need for a healthy diversity of worshipping communities integrated around our parishes to reach new and different people. We need a rich diversity of church life that reflects the rich diversity of social and cultural life in the twenty-first century in a place like London. Interestingly, on the sixth floor where my flat is situated in the new Redrow development in Colindale Gardens, our neighbours one side are from Iran, our neighbours the other side were originally two girls from Chile working as teachers and now a Christian couple from Hong Kong who attend a Chinese speaking church, the flat opposite us is owned by a lady from Hong Kong who plans eventually to settle in London and then the other end are a couple with a young daughter, both part Nigerian, but the husband's mother is Scottish and the wife's mother is Swiss. A truly cosmopolitan floor!

I believe that London is unique and mission strategies that can be seen working effectively in this multi-cultural metropolis would not necessarily work well in other dioceses and so I think it isn't easy to apply lessons from London diocese to other parts of the Church of England. In London it seems possible to have a mixed ecology that honours both the parish system but also fresh expressions of Church and there are the financial and people resources for it to be a realistic vision. I fear that in many other parts of the Church of England, especially post-Covid, it would have to be either/or and too great an emphasis on fresh expressions of church might only lead to a weakening of the life of the parish church especially in rural areas. This seems to have been a threat in Winchester diocese that resulted in the resignation of the diocesan bishop and also has led to concerns being voiced in Leicester diocese, where the bishop, interestingly, was a for a short-time my successor as Bishop of Tewkesbury but wasn't in Gloucester diocese long enough to appreciate and understand some of the unique challenges and opportunities of mission and ministry where a significant part of the life of a diocese is made up of small communities each with their own parish church. Interestingly, a former student of mine from Wycliffe Hall formerly Bishop of Truro has been appointed the new Bishop of Winchester. Church Press coverage of his appointment reveals a certain element of disquiet about whether he may wish to pursue the policies of the former Bishop of Winchester though from my knowledge of him I believe his leadership style would be more consultative and consensual!

The death of Queen Elizabeth II in September 2022 and her subsequent lying in state in Westminster Hall and her funeral in Westminster Abbey seemed to offer evidence that though the number of people attending church on a Sunday is considerably less than 50 years ago or even 10 years ago, a much larger group of people still exhibit an innate spirituality that finds expression in prayerfulness even if not in attending a service in a church on a regular basis. If those spiritually open people are ever to be reached and enabled to embrace the Christian faith and grow into discipleship, there will need to continue to be a physical church presence in communities of all sizes up and down the country with a group of Christians meeting for worship and teaching.

A potential knock-on effect of the Covid pandemic on the role of the parish church was the closure of churches for a long period during the pandemic. Angela Tilby reflected on this in her column in the *Church Times* for 17 March, 2023. She pointed out that the closure of churches was not mandated directly by government. It was the Church leaders who made the decision. She argues that they were probably influenced in their decision by the fear that if there were an outbreak of Covid linked to a church, the Church of England would end up being blamed. Interestingly, I myself succumbed to Covid twice in spite of being up to date with all the available vaccines. The first occasion I picked it up was Holy Week 2022 after sharing with the local Methodist church for a Palm Sunday service which I was leading and so I felt the need to stay behind after the service for coffee and fellowship with our Methodist neighbours! One of them kindly passed Covid on to me! Angela Tilby argues that the draconian closure of all churches was in her view wrong. She points out that even in times of disaster church buildings have always remained open and been a sign of visible solidarity with the sick and the dying. Evidently a report by the University of York suggested that 75% of non-church members wanted access to churches during the pandemic as places of quiet reflection and comfort. She continues: "I cannot get out of my mind the memory of a desperate man hammering on the closed doors of our cathedral in Portsmouth shortly after the announcement of church closures. In that decision some of the poorest and most vulnerable members of the community lost their place of sanctuary."

Historically, churches have remained open as places for anyone, whether having faith or no faith, to be able to slip into in order to sit and quietly pray or simply be open to the presence and love of God. In more recent times because of the risk of theft or vandalism many churches, especially in urban and inner-city areas, have been closed midweek. One of the good things about churches in Gloucestershire during my time there as Bishop of Tewkesbury was that the majority of the rural churches remained open during daylight hours seven days a week. Also when I was House for Duty priest in Latimer, I insisted on the church being kept open and from entries in the visitors' book it was clear that a large number of people greatly valued finding the church open and appreciated the beautiful sense of peace pervading the building. All this is additional evidence for the importance of a church at the heart of every community however small that community, however small the regular congregation.

Chapter 11

Further Reflections on a Distinctive Anglican Ecclesiology

Lambeth Conferences

As Bishop of Tewkesbury, I was privileged to attend two Lambeth Conferences, the first in 1998 when George Carey was Archbishop of Canterbury and the second in 2008 when Rowan Williams was Archbishop of Canterbury. As mentioned in an earlier chapter, the first Lambeth Conference was held in 1867 as a forum for fellowship and study and seeking to hold together in unity a broad spectrum of churches across the world. It was called by Archbishop Longley in the light of issues raised by the publication of Essays and Reviews in 1860 where traditional views of the authority of Scripture were challenged and issues also raised by the "unorthodox" views of Colenso, Bishop of Natal, about the Pentateuch. From the earliest days it was agreed that any resolutions passed by Lambeth Conferences did not have the authority of Papal Encyclicals but were simply an attempt to give expression to views seen as expressive of Anglicanism and to seek to hold diverse churches together in some kind of unity.

The Lambeth Conferences came to be held usually every ten years; the Lambeth Conference that was due to be held in 2018 was postponed to give more time to attempt to resolve the deepening divide within the Anglican Communion over same-sex relationships and then the Covid pandemic intervened so the Lambeth Conference due in 2018 eventually took place in 2022. Though in earlier times there were tensions and disagreements, these became more sharply drawn and serious in the early twenty-first century and potentially disruptive of the unity of the Anglican Church. At the 2008 Lambeth Conference some

200 Bishops (mostly from African provinces, Sydney and the Southern Cone and including the Primates of Nigeria, Uganda, Rwanda, Kenya and Tanzania) absented themselves, holding an alternative Conference in Jerusalem under the title of GAFCON.

There was some improvement in relationships between bishops holding polarised views since the 2008 Lambeth Conference. Dr Idowu-Fearon, the retiring Secretary General of the Anglican Communion, wrote in the *Church Times* of 24 September, 2021, an article with the heading "Anglicans now less rancorous". He pointed out that at the time of Archbishop Justin Welby's installation in 2012 several Primates were absenting themselves from the Primates' Meetings. At the time of his article all but three Primates were attending those meetings. Dr Idowu-Fearon suggested that this positive outcome was largely due to Archbishop Welby having made personal visits to each of the Primates early on in his time as Archbishop of Canterbury. Dr Idowu-Fearon in that article acknowledged that the divisions haven't disappeared but that there is "very little of the bitterness and rancour that existed previously".

Since Dr Idowu-Fearon wrote that article, sadly the potential for deeper divisions in the Anglican Communion has increased. The General Synod of the Church of England met in February 2023 and approved a proposal to bless same-sex civil marriages. Other Provinces in the past have approved same-sex marriages but the Archbishop of Canterbury is in a unique position as viewed as "head" of the Anglican Communion and the focus of unity within the Communion. As a result of that decision by General Synod, a large number of African Provinces have declared that they no longer acknowledge that they are in communion with the Archbishop of Canterbury. In the *Church Times* of 3 March, 2023, there was an article headed "London Conservatives turn to GAFCON". A large number of Evangelical clergy and parishes in London diocese have declared their intention to seek alternative episcopal oversight. An indication of the depth of the divisions is seen in the fact that large numbers of lay people and clergy in the Church of England are angry that Synod and the House of Bishops are not prepared to agree to the Church marrying gay couples while large numbers of other lay people and clergy are angry that the Church is prepared to bless gay marriages.

Reconciliation at the Heart of the Gospel

Archbishop Justin Welby brought with him as Archbishop a strong history of involvement in reconciliation through his links with Coventry Cathedral. He was a Canon of Coventry Cathedral from 2002–2007 and from 2002–2005 he was involved in their international ministry with its strong emphasis on the work of reconciliation. In an interview with Dr Paula Gooder hosted by St Paul's Cathedral (following the Archbishop's Sabbatical where he spent time reflecting further on reconciliation and writing a book on that theme) he was asked for a succinct definition of reconciliation. This was his reply to Paula: "Reconciliation is the transformation of broken and destructive relationships into accepting diversity with love." During that interview he also reflected on a statement made by Sam Wells, Vicar of St Martins-in-the-Field, at a conference on Reconciliation hosted by Coventry Cathedral during his time there as a Canon, that the "gospel is reconciliation and reconciliation is the gospel". The main divisive issue within the Anglican Communion though not the only potentially divisive issue has been sexual ethics and not doctrinal though some would argue that it isn't possible to separate doctrinal and ethical issues, that they are interrelated.

During my time as Vice-Principal at Wycliffe Hall Theological College, I took my turn one term as a staff member giving a series of Bible Studies at one of the mid-week evening services on St Paul's Second Letter to the Corinthians. As I spent several weeks in the Bodleian Library reading commentaries on 2 Corinthians in preparation for writing my biblical expositions, I found myself very much drawn to the theme of Reconciliation as being at the heart of the gospel especially in the light of 2 Corinthians 5, 19–20: "All things flow from God who has reconciled us to himself through Christ and given us the ministry of reconciliation, namely that God was in Christ reconciling the world to himself, not reckoning people's transgressions against them and placing among us the message of reconciliation" (my own translation: the Greek implies that the community of Christians is not simply to proclaim that message of reconciliation which is at the heart of the gospel but to live it out, to be a living visual aid of reconciliation). During my time on the staff of Wycliffe Hall Theological College there were some very sad divisions between students holding polarised views on some issues as referred to in an earlier chapter. All such divisions run the risk of undermining the message of reconciliation that is to be lived out among Christians who may not always agree.

On one occasion when I was Bishop of Tewkesbury, the Director of Ministerial Training had asked me to offer a biblical reflection on the set New Testament reading for Evening Prayer at the end of a day conference for clergy. The set reading that weekday was the second letter of John. I had never preached on 2 John and I enjoyed reading around that short letter and reflecting on the relationship between Truth and Love. The letter focuses equally on both as important to Christians. The letter opens: "To the lady chosen by God and to her children, whom I love in the truth – and not I only, but also all who know the truth because of the truth which lives in us and will be with us for ever." The letter goes on to say in verses 4 and 5: "It has given me great joy to find some of your children walking in the truth, just as the Father commanded us. And now, dear lady, I am not writing you a new commandment but one we have had from the beginning. I ask that we love one another. And this is love: that we walk in obedience to his commands. As you have heard from the beginning, his command is that you walk in love." Truth and Love were perfectly held together by Jesus during his earthly ministry but his followers have never found it easy to hold them together in perfect complementarity and while some Christians are strong on Truth but weak on Love, other Christians are strong on Love, but weak on Truth. As an Evangelical I believe strongly that Truth matters, but I also acknowledge that at the heart of my Christian faith is the statement, again in the writings of John, that God is love and we find that love perfectly expressed in the Person of Jesus Christ.

A Focus on "Generous Orthodoxy"

At the 2008 Lambeth Conference one of the optional evening addresses laid on by Archbishop Rowan Williams was an address by Brian McLaren on Generous Orthodoxy. A generous orthodoxy invites Christians of different persuasions to embrace a radical, Christ-centred orthodoxy of faith and practice in a missional, generous spirit. Rather than seeking to offer a sharp definition of what is and what is not "orthodox", McLaren used the phrase in a book he wrote in 2004. He explores the many different traditions of faith within Christian history bringing to the centre a way of life that draws us closer to Christ and to each other. Such an approach is potentially helpful in ecumenical discussions, but is also helpful in holding together a measure of unity in a richly diverse Anglican Communion. This was undoubtedly why Archbishop Rowan invited McLaren to address us Bishops at the 2008 Lambeth Conference, though, of course, sadly some who might have benefited from hearing him speak and taking on board his views had absented themselves from the Conference, choosing instead to set up GAFCON as an alternative to the Lambeth Conference.

McLaren in fact was not the first person to use the term "Generous Orthodoxy". It was used by Hans Frei, a theologian at Yale Divinity School in the 1970s and 1980s. He used the phrase in an article penned in 1987 as a response to an article written by Carl Henry. Carl Henry was in a strongly Conservative Evangelical tradition; he was a signatory to the 1978 Chicago statement on biblical inerrancy and stood for a propositional approach to biblical truth. Frei in his article wrote as follows: "My own vision of what might be propitious for our day, split as we are, not so much into denominations as into two schools of thought, is that we need a kind of generous orthodoxy which would have in it an element of liberalism and an element of evangelicalism." The reference to liberalism could be misunderstood. A better phrase to describe what Frei meant could be a humble acknowledgement of the place of mystery in talking about God, a recognition that the truth about God is beyond our best attempts to give expression to that truth. Frei, interestingly, from an Anglican perspective saw generous orthodoxy rooted in the historic credal faith of the early Church. He was certainly opposed to a liberalism which when a conviction held by Christians doesn't fit in with the prevailing worldview of the day quickly reinterprets it to fit in with contemporary culture.[15]

Ordination Training: Course or College?

St Mellitus College during my time as Bishop was set up to train ordinands for ordination in the Church of England and became increasingly popular among ordinands of a wide cross-section of traditions. When St Mellitus was set up in 2007, a Memorandum of intent was drawn up outlining the agreement for the new College. The Memorandum included the following statement: "The Bishops and Dean of St Mellitus will ensure that the College provides a training that represents a generous Christian orthodoxy and that trains ordinands in such a way that all mainstream traditions of the Church have proper recognition and provision within the training."

Church of England Theological Colleges arose in the nineteenth century representing different theological traditions within the Church of England and inevitably perpetuated those distinct traditions. This was partly because the bishops in the nineteenth century didn't see the need for colleges to be set up to train ordinands. The custom had been for a bishop simply to meet with an ordinand and give him (only men at that time) a reading list and then ordain him. Others representing different traditions believed that this was inadequate and so took steps to set up colleges and set them up within their own theological traditions. Increasingly during the second half of the twentieth century it was felt especially by bishops that it would be better for ordinands of different theological traditions to be trained alongside each other, learning from one another.

As Bishop of Tewkesbury I chaired the Governing Body of WEMTC (West of England Ministerial Training Course) in the 1990s and early twenty-first century and I found that those from a definite Evangelical background who trained on WEMTC instead of going to an Evangelical College generally emerged (there were occasional exceptions of some who by interacting with people seen by them as unhelpfully "liberal" became even more confirmed in their conservative views through interaction with theological views they saw as almost "heretical"!) at the end of training with a better understanding of traditions different from their own, a healthy respect for those traditions and a willingness to learn from them.

There were also practical factors requiring the provision of non-residential training in areas local to the ordinands. When I trained for ordination in the 1960s, the majority of ordinands were young single men and so there were no practical issues involved in uprooting ordinands from their local area to train residentially. There was a monastic feel to training at that time – a group of men sharing a common life separated from the world. However, during the 1970s and 1980s increasingly those offering for ordination were older, often married, sometimes with a family and from a practical point of view it was more acceptable not to uproot the family, but to allow the ordinands to continue in their secular employment, training non-residentially and in their local home setting. As women began to be trained in equal numbers again from a practical point of view non-residential training was more suitable. However, the main benefit of training people of different theological traditions alongside each other was not a purely practical one but as mentioned above encouraging people to be open to theological views different from their own and a willingness to learn from each other.

Those responsible for setting up St Mellitus were concerned to break the mould of previous theological training within colleges representing a very specific theological position. There was a recognition that training alongside like-minded ordinands ran the risk of reinforcing unhelpful stereotypes and also fostering suspicion of those holding different theological views. It was Simon Downham, at the time Vicar of St Paul's, Hammersmith, who suggested the phrase "Generous Orthodoxy" to describe the distinctive approach to training offered by St Mellitus.

Those of a more Conservative Evangelical persuasion or Anglo-Catholic Traditionalists might argue that such an approach runs the risk of shaping people in a lowest common denominator; however, my own conviction is that such an approach at its best enables a willingness to respect traditions different from one's own and a willingness to learn from different traditions and be enriched by insights from those other traditions. This again seems to me to be something that characterises an Anglican Evangelical over against Evangelicals standing more in a Free Church tradition and acknowledges those theological truths at the heart of the Anglican tradition of a comprehensive Church whose theological understanding recognises a dispersed rather than a single approach to authority in the Church.

A Dispersed Approach to Authority

Unlike the Roman Catholic Church with authority invested in the Pope and Papal Encyclicals and unlike some Protestant Churches that appeal solely to Scripture, the Anglican approach has involved an appeal to dispersed authority. There are various places where such an approach can be found within Anglican documents. Bishops of the Episcopal Church of the USA gathered at Chicago in 1884 issued a document that was concerned with finding a basis for Ecumenical unity. This document was taken up at the 1888 Lambeth Conference as a basis for any future reunion of Churches. It included the following four criteria:

(i) The Holy Scriptures of the Old and New Testaments as "containing all things necessary to salvation" and as being the rule and ultimate standard of faith

(ii) The Apostles Creed as the Baptismal Symbol and the Nicene Creed as the sufficient statement of the Christian faith

(iii) The two Sacraments ordained by Christ himself – Baptism and the Supper of the Lord – ministered with unfailing use of Christ's words of Institution and of the elements ordained by him

(iv) The Historic Episcopate, locally adapted in the method of its administration to the varying needs of the nations and peoples called of God into the Unity of his Church.

The first three points seem to me to provide a distinctively Anglican approach to authority embracing the priority of Scripture but also giving space to an appropriate acceptance of Tradition and also to the Sacramental life of the Church. The fourth point acknowledges a place for a degree of variety in the light of different contexts which is significant and takes us into the realm of hermeneutics and could potentially leave the door open to recognise that Anglican Churches in different social and cultural contexts might come to hold different views on some ethical issues and that it might be possible for them to coexist harmoniously.

Another statement is the Declaration of Assent as revised in 1975 which clergy at their ordination and all clergy entering on a new post have to affirm:

> The Church of England is part of the One, Holy, Catholic and Apostolic Church worshipping the one true God, Father, Son and Holy Spirit. It professes the faith uniquely revealed in the Holy Scriptures and set forth in the Catholic creeds, which faith the Church is called upon to proclaim afresh in each generation. Led by the Holy Spirit it has borne witness to Christian truth in its historic formularies, the Thirty-nine Articles of Religion, the Book of Common Prayer and the Ordering of Bishops, Priests and Deacons.

The Declaration of Assent also gives expression to a variety of sources of authority for belief over against Sola Scriptura though recognising the supreme authority of Scripture. It also acknowledges a place for ongoing reinterpretation of our understanding of truth in the light of changing social and cultural factors.

As mentioned in my opening chapter Sola Scriptura was indeed a watch word of the Reformation and many have taken that as excluding all other sources for our understanding of Christian truth but that does not, as I have mentioned in an earlier chapter, seem to me to be the position adopted by Anglicans. Another way of viewing Sola Scriptura, as again mentioned before, is to see it as referring to the basis of our salvation; that our understanding of the grounds for being "saved" is found in Scripture alone. Similarly when references are made to *the plain sense of Scripture*, that is not to be understood as an all-embracing term implying that we can find answers to all issues and questions as Christians simply by reading them off the pages of the Bible, but rather that the Bible is crystal clear over the issue of how a person can discover and enjoy a relationship with the living God, Father, Son and Holy Spirit, the basis of our salvation. It leaves the door open to wrestling with issues of interpretation on a whole host of issues where the Bible for better or worse is far from conveying a plain sense, convincing to all Christians. So Christians can disagree and clearly have disagreed, for example, over the practice of Baptism (Infant or Believers' Baptism) and over the gifts of the Holy Spirit and over the ministry of women in the Church to take just three examples.

Again, as mentioned in my opening chapter Infant Baptism is an interesting example where for Anglicans tradition plays a part. As an Evangelical Anglican I am persuaded that on balance there is New Testament support for baptising babies, though not conclusive; reading the Acts of the Apostles on its own I would have to acknowledge that there is more evidence for Believers' Baptism. However, I also recognise that there is abundant evidence of Infant Baptism from earliest times in the practice of the undivided Church, the place of Tradition complementing the evidence of Scripture. Polycarp Bishop of Smyrna was martyred in 155 AD; the Proconsul tried to persuade him to "swear by the genius of Caesar". Polycarp's reply was as follows: "eighty and six years have I served him and he hath done me no wrong; how then can I blaspheme my king who saved me?" It is very unlikely that Polycarp was over 86 years old at this time and so his reference to serving Christ for 86 years most likely is dated back to his baptism as a baby or a very young child. Polycarp is just one of several individuals called on by Jeremias in his book on Infant Baptism in the first four centuries to confirm the existence of infant baptism from earliest times in the history of the Christian Church.[16]

Again, I repeat a view stated in my opening chapter that as far as gifts of the Holy Spirit are concerned I would as an Evangelical Anglican hold together both the teaching of the New Testament and the experience of Charismatic Christians in the Church of England and elsewhere in the Anglican Communion from the second half of the twentieth century alongside the experience of African-American Christians in the Azusa Street Revival that took place from 1906. Pentecostal Christians often argue that "this is that", in other words that their experience of the Holy Spirit is equivalent to the experience of the first Christians as recorded in the Acts of the Apostles and promised by Jesus to his followers: "You will be baptised in the Holy Spirit." Interestingly, the importance of that promise of Jesus is underlined by being repeated several times in the pages of the New Testament in different New Testament books. The Anglican inclusion of *consensus fidelium* would support such an approach to belief about the place of the Holy Spirit in the community of faith.

Though some Evangelicals argue that the Reformation set the Church of England in a totally Protestant and Reformed tradition, my own view is that the Reformers were keen to affirm that the Church of England was not simply Reformed but Catholic and Reformed. So I recognise that from our foundations there is a breadth contained within the Church of England that as Evangelicals we need to acknowledge and respect. Such an understanding of the Church of England being Reformed and Catholic is found in the writings of Hooker, often seen as *The Father of Anglicanism*. Hooker offers in my view a distinctively Anglican understanding of the Church. Writing at the end of the sixteenth century in his classic work *The Laws of Ecclesiastic Polity* he offers a via media understanding of the Church that is opposed to Catholic ecclesiology on the one hand but is also opposed to Puritan views and yet seeks to embrace both Reformed and Catholic understandings.

Sykes comments on Hooker's phrase *the essence of Christianity* which he identifies with the *regula fidei*[17] The early Fathers, e.g., Tertullian, Irenaeus and others used this phrase to give expression to those beliefs which "Orthodox" Christians held in common and came to be summarised in the Apostles' Creed and the Nicene Creed. During subsequent centuries the Church in both the West and the East added many other doctrines which the Reformers rejected as going beyond and incompatible with the essence of the Christian faith as expressed in Scripture and the early Creeds. In affirming these early Creeds alongside Scripture, Hooker adopted a different stance to those of a more Puritan tradition. In his writings we find a distinctively Anglican ecclesiology as a commitment to hold together in complementarity both Catholic and also Protestant/Reformed understandings. Anglicans, I believe, take seriously the early history of the undivided Church.

Interestingly, when I was Vicar of Holy Trinity, Margate, a woman in the congregation had lively discussions with me. She took a stand on Sola Scriptura and disagreed with certain decisions I took as not found in scripture. She was quite happy totally to ignore 2000 years of Church history. In my view we cannot do that; we have to take seriously the way the life and teaching of the Church has developed over 2000 years and that in my view is the position adopted by the Anglican Church historically both at the time of the Reformation and over the years since the Reformation.

Hooker especially highlights the difference between the Reformers (often associated with Geneva and Calvin) who majored on Scripture alone and those Reformers (particularly associated with the Church of England and to some extent Luther) who found a place for Church Tradition alongside Scripture while still affirming the supremacy of Scripture. Stephen Spencer refers to a time when Hooker was preacher at the Temple Courts in London. Hooker preached in the morning while Walter Travers of a Puritan tradition preached in the evening. Together, Spencer argues, Travers and Hooker represented those two different strands within the Reformation. Travers took his stand on Scripture alone, while Hooker in contrast set alongside Scripture which as a good Protestant retained the first place both Reason and Tradition.[18]

Jaroslav Pelican in a Lutheran tradition has written extensively on the place of Tradition in the Church's self-understanding. He penned the following memorable phrase in a 1983 Lecture: "Tradition is the living faith of the dead, traditionalism is the dead faith of the living! And I suppose I should add, it is traditionalism that gives Tradition such a bad name.[19]

As an Anglican Evangelical I am clear that Tradition has always to be subject to the priority of the testimony of Scripture. As Tradition evolved some paths can be accepted as in line with the testimony of Scripture, while other paths moved in a direction that was not consistent with Scripture. It is noteworthy that John Henry Newman who was initially identified as an Evangelical ended up being welcomed into the Roman Catholic Church as he wrestled with the nature of the relationship between Scripture and Tradition. He wrote *An Essay on the Development of Christian Doctrine* which charted his move to an acceptance of all the developments that had taken place within the Roman Catholic Church. He used an illustration of an acorn and a fully grown oak tree. The oak tree is nothing like the acorn; however, the potential for the oak tree to grow is contained within the acorn and there is an inevitable line of growth from the one to the other. There is here a certain kind of logic that is very attractive but ultimately it puts Scripture under the authority of the Church rather than an Evangelical view that the Church always needs to stand under the authority of Scripture. What if the tree that emerged from the acorn turned out to be a silver birch or an ash tree!

Ordained Ministry: Catholic and Reformed

One issue which divided the two traditions within the Reformation was the nature of ordained ministry. Hooker along with other Church of England Reformers argued in favour of a three-fold ministry of bishops, priests and deacons. The Puritans in contrast argued that there was no biblical evidence for such a threefold ministerial order. To some extent bishop (episcopos) and elder (presbyteros) seem interchangeable at times in the letters of the New Testament. Leadership generally seems to have been plural (a group of presbyters). It could be that as the church grew numerically one elder from a group of elders leading a local church was elevated to be the leader, episcopos (bishop); so a model of a bishop exercising leadership in partnership with a group of elders. Deacons appear to have been a distinctive order of ministry rather than a stepping stone to presbyteral ministry as happened later in the development of church structures. As an Evangelical I have to admit that the three-fold ministry of bishops, priests (presbyters) and deacons cannot be clearly established on the basis of the New Testament evidence alone, but it came to be the universal practice of the undivided Church very early on and is certainly not incompatible with the testimony of the New Testament. Again, this is an example of Tradition drawing out Scriptural testimony.

Ministerial issues also highlight the diversity within Anglicanism in relation to bishops. It is possible historically to identify three distinct positions in relation to Episcopacy: that bishops are of the **esse** of the Church (no bishop, no Church, a tradition going back at least to Cyprian), or the **plene esse** (for a Church to be fully the Church you need bishops, a view compatible with the fourth criterion in the 1888 Lambeth Statement about a basis for the reunion of the Churches) or the **bene esse** of the Church (a good and helpful ministry, but not essential for a Church to be identified as a Church). Many

Anglican Evangelicals have argued in favour of the third view, whereas my own view is that as an Anglican Evangelical a more appropriate view in keeping with belonging to the Anglican Church is that bishops are of the **plene esse** of the Church, though some of my Evangelical friends would probably say that I would be expected to hold that view as a bishop!

As Anglicans in the twenty-first century as well as going back to our foundational statements at the time of the Reformation, I believe we need to take seriously how Anglicanism has taken shape over the centuries. In its unfolding history at different times there have been different emphases contributing to shaping the Church as we experience it in the twenty-first century. The Evangelical Revival is part of that history, as too is the Oxford Movement, as too is the Charismatic Renewal of the twentieth century and as too is an Anglican emphasis on leaving space for the place of Reason in the exploration of theology.

It is true that over against Roman Catholic theology, at the time the Reformers laid a special emphasis on the Word of God as constitutive of the Church. Paul Avis in his book *The Church in the theology of the Reformers* argues that for Luther the "gospel alone when believed constitutes and creates the Church". His summary of the thought of the Reformers on the Church is that "the Word is all determinative for the being of the Church. It creates and builds the Church and gives life to its varied ministries".[20] In the twentieth century P T Forsyth majored on the Church as "the creature of the preached gospel of God's grace". Famously too Karl Barth in his 1921 edition of his commentary on Paul's Letter to the Romans referred to the Church as "no more than a crater formed by the explosion of a shell, the gospel". The Church of England Article 19 of the 39 Articles of the Church expresses it this way:

> The visible Church of Christ is a congregation of faithful men [sic], in the which the pure Word of God is preached

and the Sacraments be duly ministered according to Church ordinance. Article 5 Of the Sufficiency of the Holy Scriptures for Salvation states that Holy Scripture contains all things necessary to Salvation, so that whatsoever is not read therein, nor may be proved thereby, is not to be required of any man that it should be believed as an article of the Faith.

Together these two Articles spell out the primary place of Scripture in an Anglican understanding of the nature of the Church. As an Evangelical I rejoice to have such a clear statement as foundational to the Church of England's self-understanding and self-identity.

For a more Catholic understanding I turn to Michael Ramsey in his classic book: *The Gospel and the Catholic Church*. He writes about a church structure evolving very early on and "this structure grows and it takes the form of an organism of Sacraments, Episcopacy, Scripture and the Creeds. This Order has persisted; it existed through all Christendom for fifteen centuries and in a large part of Christendom it exists today".[21] As an Anglican Evangelical I believe it is important to hold together in complementarity both understandings of the Church.

A Search for a "Pure" Church

This dispersed approach to authority has in my view marked off Anglican Evangelicals from Free Church Evangelicals. John Stott as Rector of All Souls, Langham Place, was an extremely influential figure in the world of Anglican Evangelicals. A key moment for Anglican Evangelicals took place in October 1966. Martin Lloyd-Jones, Minister at Westminster Chapel, was a leading Free Church Evangelical and was invited to give an address at the second National Assembly of Evangelicals (the first had taken place the previous year). The Assembly was chaired by John Stott. In his address Martin Lloyd-Jones passionately pleaded for all Evangelicals to leave their "corrupt" churches and come together to form a pan-Evangelical Fellowship, a visible rather than a purely spiritual unity. After he had spoken, John Stott as chairman offered a robust challenge to Martin Lloyd-Jones. At some length he argued that both history and Scripture were opposed to Martin Lloyd-Jones's arguments. It was a key moment for Anglican Evangelicals encouraged by John Stott to remain within the Church of England and to pray and work for change within it. Though a few Anglican Evangelical clergy left the Church of England between 1966 and 1974, it was only a handful and John Stott's arguments won the day.

There is a strong tradition of a "mixed" view of the Church based on the parable of the wheat and the tares in the teaching of Jesus and forcefully argued for by Saint Augustine at the time of the Donatist controversy. During a period of fierce persecution with Christians facing martyrdom, some clergy and bishops compromised their Christian faith to avoid martyrdom. When the period of persecution was over the Church was prepared to welcome back into the church those who had "betrayed" their Christian faith. The Donatists refused to accept the validity of sacraments performed by those who had denied their Christian faith to avoid martyrdom. Augustine writing on Baptism (iv.16.18) "Anyone who is on the devil's side cannot defile the sacrament which is of Christ ... When baptism is administered in the words of the gospel, however great be the perverseness of either minister or recipient, the sacrament itself is holy on his account whose sacrament it is."[22] The position adopted by Saint Augustine was taken by the Anglican Reformers at the time of the Reformation. So Article 26 of the Church of England 39 Articles of Religion deals with "The unworthiness of the Ministers which hinders not the effect of the Sacrament". The Article states the following:

> Although in the visible Church the evil be ever mingled
> with the good and sometimes the evil have chief authority

in the Ministration of the Word and Sacraments, yet forasmuch as they do not the same in their own name, but in Christ's, and do minister by his commission and authority, we may use their Ministry, both in hearing the Word of God and in receiving the Sacraments. Neither is the effect of Christ's ordinance taken away by their wickedness, nor the grace of God's gifts diminished from such as by faith, and rightly, do receive the Sacraments ministered unto them; which be effectual, because of Christ's institution and promise, although they be ministered by evil men.

There have always been those attracted to the idea of a "pure" Church, but as John Stott argued persuasively back in 1966 Scripture and history suggest that there can never be a totally pure Church. Because the Church is made up of sinful men and women there will always be imperfections in the Church.

This Anglican view of the Church inherited from Saint Augustine has some relevance I believe in the controversy facing the Anglican Church at this time. Interestingly, when the story broke of General Synod agreeing to services of blessing for same-sex marriages a Baptist friend whom I got to know when I was House for Duty priest in Latimer (he is a member of Gold Hill Baptist Church) assumed I would want to separate myself from the Church of England. Also, two long-standing Methodist friends (he was a Methodist Minister and she was a Methodist Lay Preacher) both resigned from the Methodist Church over their decision about same-sex marriage. Believing that we shall never this side of eternity have a "pure" Church, I find myself at odds with those Anglican Evangelicals that see the need to seek alternative Episcopal oversight and distance themselves from the Anglican Communion. I feel sad that a significant number of bishops and primates in the Anglican Communion feel unable to accept the authority of Justin Welby any longer as Archbishop of Canterbury.

A helpful phrase that reminds us that the Church is always in need of reformation is *ecclesia semper reformanda*. This encourages us, however strong our convictions, to hold them with graciousness and humility. In my view John Stott was a wonderful example of a man of very strong convictions, but those convictions were held with humility and enormous grace.

Comprehensiveness as a Characteristic of Anglican Theology

Alongside a focus on dispersed authority, Anglican ecclesiology has also emphasised **Comprehensiveness**. Comprehensiveness inevitably follows on dispersed authority. When belief draws on a rich variety of sources of authority, conclusions reached by different members of the Church will inevitably be influenced by the particular mix of sources of authority and varying weight attributed to the different sources.

A document was published in 2020: *What do Anglicans Believe?* It is a helpful synthesis of Anglican and Ecumenical Statements on a range of doctrinal issues. It quotes from Resolution 9 of the 1920 Lambeth Conference: "it is through a rich diversity of life and devotion that the unity of the whole fellowship will be fulfilled." At one level this suggests that a distinctively Anglican understanding of the Church has a breadth about it that embraces Evangelical/Reformed and Catholic understandings. It is often claimed that Anglicans seek to regard opposing views as complementary rather than irreconcilable leading to division; opposing views held, however uncomfortably, alongside each other.

Stephen Sykes reflects that "Comprehensiveness in the context of a church means simply that the church contains in itself many elements regarded as mutually exclusive in other communions".[23] Sykes acknowledges that there are limits to diversity. So at the time of the Reformation, the Church of England felt unable to include those of a more Puritan tradition that believed that the Church of England had not been sufficiently faithful to the Scriptures. The Reformers also rejected many doctrines developed by the Roman Catholic Church down the centuries which they regarded as incompatible with Scripture. So Anglicans accept that there are limits to comprehensiveness. The so-called Chicago-Lambeth Quadrilateral, already referred to, is the primary reference point and working document for Anglicans in Ecumenical relationships, the non-negotiable areas for any reunited church and so by implication are relevant for preserving the unity of the Anglican Communion. Alongside a commitment to the authority of Scripture, the acceptance of the Apostles and Nicene Creeds and the two Sacraments instituted by Christ there is a commitment to the historic Episcopate. So the comprehensiveness of the Anglican Church does not include those who reject episcopacy and this proved a stumbling block in Anglican-Methodist conversations at various times.

As Bishop of Tewkesbury, I was privileged to take the lead in developing a relationship between the Diocese of Gloucester and two dioceses in the Church of South India, Karnataka Central diocese and Dornakal diocese where earlier in the twentieth century, Bishop Azariah was the first Indian Bishop and deeply committed to ecumenism. The United Church of South India came into existence in September 1947 and was a union of Anglican, Methodist, Presbyterian, Reformed and Congregational Churches; drawing together these different denominations with different ecclesiologies, there was a recognition that the Church needs to embrace episcopal, presbyterian and congregational elements in its life. Interestingly, as we spent time in India worshipping in different Indian churches it was usually possible to discern whether the particular united congregation had originally been Anglican or Methodist or Congregational. Also, though the Church of South

India (CSI) is an impressive expression of how Church unity can be achieved, the Baptists were not included and of course neither were Roman Catholics.

Sykes quotes a definition of comprehensiveness from one of the Reports of the 1968 Lambeth Conference:

> Comprehensiveness demands agreement on fundamentals while tolerating disagreement on matters in which Christians may disagree without feeling the necessity of breaking communion. In the mind of an Anglican comprehensiveness is not compromise.... It is not a sophisticated word for syncretism. Rather it implies that the apprehension of truth is a growing thing; we only gradually succeed in "knowing the truth".[24]

As already mentioned, comprehensiveness is understood to embrace both Reformed and Catholic understandings of the Church and the Faith. Sykes also argues that contradictory understandings are held alongside each other without being fully reconciled; such reconciliation lies in the future and so there is a reference to only gradually succeeding in knowing the truth.

As mentioned in an earlier chapter when I was Archdeacon of Surrey, I was privileged to spend three months at Tantur, the Roman Catholic Ecumenical centre in Jerusalem. I spent my time writing an article that was subsequently published in the Roman Catholic Ecumenical Journal *One in Christ* with the title "Koinonia: A Significant Milestone on the Road to Unity". My focus was on broader ecumenical relationships but because of the rich diversity within Anglicanism, the issues relevant to ecumenical relationships are also very relevant to holding the Anglican Communion in unity. Dr Mary Tanner, a leading Ecumenical Scholar described *Koinonia* as providing an opportunity for gathering the different parts of the jigsaw into a coherent whole so there emerges a "mobilising vision", a "portraiture" of the unity of the church.

With the "conversion" of the Roman Emperor Constantine, the Church and the Roman Empire became intimately connected and as a result ecclesiology majored on the Church as an Institution and Church Unity has been understood, certainly within Roman Catholic and Orthodox circles in institutional terms. However, Vatican II documents offered a different model for understanding the Church. Preliminary papers for Vatican II started with a long section on the hierarchy of the Church. However, the final form of the Vatican II documents opened with an emphasis on the Church as the people of God. The 1985 Synod of Roman Catholic Bishops made it clear that for them an "ecclesiology of Communion (koinonia) is the central and fundamental idea of the Vatican II documents". Cardinal Willebrands writing in *One in Christ* in 1974/5 on the Future of Ecumenism remarked on an ecclesiology of Communion as the focus of Vatican II and as a central insight for the future of ecumenism.

I mentioned in an earlier chapter that during our time at Tantur, though the Warden, Tom Stransky, didn't approve of an open eucharistic table between the different denominations each group of students was allowed to vote on whether to have an open table and our group voted in favour. The Report on the Process and Responses to the Ecumenical Document Baptism Eucharist and Ministry identified as a key issue whether we agree in truth and then unite or unite and discover truth on the way. I argued in my article that a *koinonia* model with its emphasis on unity in diversity is strongly supportive of the latter way forward. Roman Catholics and Orthodox Churches have seen unity at the eucharistic table as the goal of the journey towards unity. However, Henrich Fries has asked why in the light of the fragility of all unity, we should not have eucharistic fellowship as a way of anticipating final and complete unity.[25]

The official Anglican view (e.g., expressed at the 1930 Lambeth Conference) has viewed eucharistic fellowship along Roman Catholic and Orthodox lines as the goal of unity yet very many Anglicans have followed the normal practice of Protestants and practised an open eucharistic table. That has always been my own practice in ministry.

Trinitarian Theology as a Model for Unity in Diversity
Related to a focus on Koinonia, another characteristic of Anglican theology especially in the twentieth century has been a focus on Trinitarian theology. Such an emphasis is something that Anglicans share with the Orthodox. John Zizioulas in 1985 published a significant book on studies in Personhood and the Church under the title *Being in Communion*. His book draws heavily on the writings of the early Fathers (something that the Church of England Reformers accepted as significant for understanding our Christian faith). In a chapter on "Christ, the Spirit and the Church" he contrasts Western theology's (for example, of St Athanasius) focus on ontology (to do with essential being) with Eastern theology's (for example, Basil) unhappiness with ontological categories and preferring to focus on Koinonia or Communion. He sees the nature of God essentially as a communion of persons.[26] In his first letter, St John (1 John 1, 3) links the communion that Christians enjoy with one another with the communion that they enjoy with God (Father and Son); in John's gospel the communion is widened out to embrace Father, Son and Holy Spirit. The early Fathers used the word perichoresis for the interplay of the three persons of the Trinity; the word conveys a sense of the three persons of the Trinity dancing round one another! Orthodox Trinitarian thought holds together both three distinct Persons of the Trinity and the Unity of the Godhead. As a model for ecclesiology, it allows for diversity within unity. Zizioulas's significant book has implications too for broader ecumenical relationships.

In this same chapter Zizioulas also applies this relational understanding of the Trinity to the relationship between the local and the universal Church and in a way that is helpfully suggestive for ecumenical relationships and for different churches across the Anglican Communion; he writes as follows: "There is one Church as there is one God. But the expression of this one Church is the communion of the many local Churches. Communion and oneness coincide in ecclesiology."[27]

Epilogue

I count it a privilege to have been called to serve as a priest in the Church of England in the second part of the twentieth century and the early years of the twenty-first century and to have exercised such a variety of ministries and to have had links with the wider Anglican Communion. I am grateful for the countless colleagues in ministry including those in the Church of South India through our diocesan links when I was Bishop of Tewkesbury and the countless lay Christians who have enriched my spiritual life, challenged me, opened up new vistas for my faith and understanding. I am also immensely grateful for the fellowship I have been privileged to enjoy with Christians from other denominations and especially clergy and lay people in the Roman Catholic church who have opened me up to a broader vision of Christian truth and spirituality.

Within worldwide Anglicanism there are richly varied theological views which inevitably struggle to be held together in unity and mutual fellowship. Similarly, within the Church of England there is a wonderfully rich variety of theological perspectives. There are four main traditions within the Church of England and the wider Anglican Communion: Evangelical, Anglo-Catholic, Charismatic, Liberal; within each of these traditions is a rich variety of different emphases which sometimes in the past have led to vigorous debate and the breaking of Christian fellowship. In my early days of Christian discipleship and ministry I saw myself as first and foremost an Evangelical and tended to sit light to the breadth found within the Church of England in which I served and which nurtured me spiritually. Though I believe that by the grace of God I was never as negative or judgemental towards those who didn't share my Evangelical faith as some of my Evangelical friends, I certainly didn't view other traditions positively and certainly was not at that time open to value them and learn from them.

Over a lifetime of discipleship and ministry for a rich variety of reasons including engaging in study of the riches of Anglican theology and ecclesiology especially as a staff member of Wycliffe Hall Theological College with responsibility for teaching ecclesiology, meeting with people of a different theological outlook to pray with them and study the scriptures with them (especially as a member of a bishop's staff team as an archdeacon and later as a bishop but also during my time as a vicar in Margate), through times of challenge and personal suffering discovering that my spiritual life was nurtured not just by the scriptures but increasingly by the sacramental life of the Church and experiencing especially in the challenges of a first incumbency in Margate the love and support of Charismatic Christians, also through times of pain and suffering and as a theological college tutor giving lectures on the philosophy of religion, and coming to acknowledge an important place for mystery and living with unanswered questions, and wanting to challenge students who too readily accepted simplistic answers to some of the major questions facing anyone who has a faith, I found the parameters of my faith wonderfully expanded and enriched.

The Charismatic movement within the Church of England became a significant factor during the 1960s through several churches such as St Mark's, Gillingham, and St Michael-le-Belfry in York. David Watson was the Vicar of St Michael-le-Belfry and during his time there the church ran renewal weeks for clergy and key lay people. Rosemary and I attended one of those weeks encouraged by a Christian doctor in the congregation in Margate who was also a licensed lay reader; the week was a time of very special spiritual blessing. David Watson was criticised in some Evangelical circles for being willing to work with Roman Catholics on mission events. He was aware of a significant movement of the Holy Spirit in Roman Catholic circles and though he would not have signed up to all Roman Catholic doctrines, he believed that it was impossible to deny the work of the Holy Spirit within Roman Catholicism. He has often been quoted as saying "All Word and no Spirit we dry up. All Spirit and no Word we blow up. When we focus on Word and Spirit together we grow up".[28] Words of great wisdom and true to an Anglican Trinitarian theology that embraces the ministry of Father, Son and Holy Spirit.

In John 17, Jesus in his High Priestly prayer prays for the unity of his followers and links the unity of his disciples with enabling an unbelieving world to discover faith in him. The early days of the Ecumenical Movement often spoke of the "scandal" of our divisions. Too easily we have as Christians accepted the inevitability of our divisions and treated them lightly. Sadly, in recent times fresh divisions have opened up within both the Church of England and the wider Anglican Communion, so the unity of both is seriously threatened. I have sought to argue in this book that there are within Anglican theology and ecclesiology truths that can enable us as Christians while holding significantly different theological and ecclesiological views to remain in fellowship with one another. Within my own Evangelical tradition there is a real tendency to fragment and to set very clear boundaries of "orthodoxy" and unchurch those who don't conform. I have sought to show that by cherishing my Evangelical convictions within an Anglican ecclesiological framework valuing the theological and ecclesiological truths that historically have been at the heart of the Anglican tradition, I have come to hold on to and appreciate a vision of a church that is united at the same time as allowing for an enormous richness of diversity. May we acknowledge the importance of striving to maintain the unity of the Spirit in the bond of peace (drawing on Ephesians 4) in order that the world may believe (John 17). In a deeply divided and fragmented world it is so important that the Church of Jesus Christ presents a model of a community of rich diversity being united in the love of God, Father, Son and Holy Spirit.

The Church of England provided reflections for each day in Lent, 2023, under the umbrella title of "Dust and Glory". The reflection for Monday, 20 March was based on words from Ephesians 3, 7–13 and included this helpful reflection on that passage:

> When we're talking about "the Church" in Ephesians, we are talking about the gathering of all God's people, called out and saved throughout all time and history to gather around the throne of Jesus, the heavenly assembly, the universal, cosmic, multi-national, multi-racial, boundary-less community of saved and reconciled people. And through the assembly of "called out" ones, the manifold wisdom of God will be made known. The "wisdom" of God is his wonderful redemption plan to unite heaven and earth, and all peoples, through the death of his Son Jesus on the Cross.

As I read those words I was reminded once again of the stunning fifteenth-century Ghent Altar piece, the painting by the Van Eyck brothers, Jan and Hubert, of *The Adoration of the Mystic Lamb*.

At the same time as well as the danger of increasing fragmentation within Anglicanism there is the danger in the Church of England of losing hold of a number of the traditions that have been at the heart of the Church of England historically such as the importance of maintaining a church presence in every community. I fully acknowledge that in our contemporary society where people relate not simply to others in a local community but through social media, they relate to others potentially on a very broad canvas and there need to be new ways of communicating the Christian good news as through fresh expressions of Church, but such Fresh Expressions in my view need to sit alongside traditional parish ministry and structures. As I mentioned before the Church of England has a noble history of being a "mixed economy" Church finding support in the New Testament in the words of St Paul writing to the young Christians in Corinth "I have become all things to all people so that by all possible means I might save some" (1 Corinthians 9, 22).

My prayer is that the Church of England may continue to shed the light of the presence of Christ to every fresh generation.

Endnotes

1. Tim Bradshaw, *The Olive Branch,* An Evangelical Anglican Doctrine of the Church (Paternoster Press, 1992) p. 138
2. Bradshaw p. 18
3. Stephen W Sykes ed., Authority in the Anglican Communion Appendix pp. 284–5
4. William Purcell, *Anglican Spirituality,* A Continuing Tradition (Mowbray, 1988) p. 27
5. The Easter Stories, (SPCK, 2008) p. 86
6. Resolution 9, subsection IV of the 1920 Lambeth Conference
7. Transforming Worship – Living a New Creation: A Report by the Liturgical Commission, GS 1651, June 2007, Section 2.8
8. GS 1651 Section 2.14 and 2.15
9. Norman Thomas, ed,. *Readings in* World Mission, (SPCK, 1995) p. 144
10. Norman Thomas, pp. 144–145
11. David J Bosch, *Transforming Mission: Paradigm Shifts in Theology of Mission,* (Orbis Books, 4th Printing) p. 405
12. Bosch p. 407
13. Kelly Whitaker, ed., *Spiritual Journeys, Poetry Today,* (Penhaligon Page Ltd, 1997) p. 157
14. TS Eliot, *Little Gidding,* Poem in Four Quartets
15. Jason A Springs, *Towards a Generous Orthodoxy: Prospects for Hans Frei's Postliberal Theology* (Footnote 48 in the Introduction, OUP, 2010)
16. Joachim Jeremias, *Infant Baptism in the First Four Centuries,* (SCM, 1960)
17. Stephen W Sykes, *The Integrity of Anglicanism,* (Seabury Press, 1978) p. 11
18. Stephen Spencer, *SCM Study Guide to* Anglicanism, (SCM, 2010) p. 141
19. Jaroslav Pelican, *The Vindication of Tradition* The 1983 *Jefferson Lecture in the Humanities*

20. Paul Avis, *The Church in the Theology of the* Reformers, (Marshall Morgan & Scott,1981) p. 1
21. Michael Ramsey, *The Gospel and the Catholic* Church, New Impression of 2nd edition (SPCK,1990) p. 57
22. Henry Bettenson, ed., *Documents of the Christian* Church, (OUP Paperback, 1989) p. 78
23. Stephen W Sykes, *The Integrity of* Anglicanism, (Seabury Press, 1978) p. 8
24. Stephen W Sykes, *The Integrity of* Anglicanism, (Seabury Press, 1978) p. 9
25. Fries and Rahner, *The Unity of the Church an Actual* Possibility, (Paulist Press,1985)
26. John D Zizioulas, *Being as* Communion, (St Vladimir's Seminary Press, 1985) p. 134
27. John D Zizioulas, p. 135.
28. David Watson, *I Believe in the Church,* (Hodder and Stoughton, 1979)

CHRISTIAN ALTERNATIVE
BOOKS

THE NEW OPEN SPACES

Throughout the two thousand years of Christian tradition there have been, and still are, groups and individuals that exist in the margins and upon the edge of faith. But in Christianity's contrapuntal history it has often been these outcasts and pioneers that have forged contemporary orthodoxy out of former radicalism as belief evolves to engage with and encompass the ever-changing social and scientific realities. Real faith lies not in the comfortable certainties of the Orthodox, but somewhere in a half-glimpsed hinterland on the dirt track to Emmaus, where the Death of God meets the Resurrection, where the supernatural Christ meets the historical Jesus, and where the revolution liberates both the oppressed and the oppressors.

Welcome to Christian Alternative ... a space at the edge where the light shines through.
If you have enjoyed this book, why not tell other readers by posting a review on your preferred book site.

Recent bestsellers from Christian Alternative are:

Bread Not Stones
The Autobiography of An Eventful Life
Una Kroll
The spiritual autobiography of a truly remarkable woman and a history of the struggle for ordination in the Church of England.
Paperback: 978-1-78279-804-0 ebook: 978-1-78279-805-7

The Quaker Way
A Rediscovery
Rex Ambler
Although fairly well known, Quakerism is not well understood. The purpose of this book is to explain how Quakerism works as a spiritual practice.
Paperback: 978-1-78099-657-8 ebook: 978-1-78099-658-5

Blue Sky God
The Evolution of Science and Christianity
Don MacGregor
Quantum consciousness, morphic fields and blue-sky thinking about God and Jesus the Christ.
Paperback: 978-1-84694-937-1 ebook: 978-1-84694-938-8

Celtic Wheel of the Year
Tess Ward
An original and inspiring selection of prayers combining Christian and Celtic Pagan traditions, and interweaving their calendars into a single pattern of prayer for every morning and night of the year.
Paperback: 978-1-90504-795-6

Christian Atheist
Belonging without Believing
Brian Mountford
Christian Atheists don't believe in God but miss him: especially the transcendent beauty of his music, language, ethics, and community.
Paperback: 978-1-84694-439-0 ebook: 978-1-84694-929-6

Compassion Or Apocalypse?
A Comprehensible Guide to the Thoughts of René Girard
James Warren
How René Girard changes the way we think about God and the Bible, and its relevance for our apocalypse-threatened world.
Paperback: 978-1-78279-073-0 ebook: 978-1-78279-072-3

Diary Of A Gay Priest
The Tightrope Walker
Rev. Dr. Malcolm Johnson
Full of anecdotes and amusing stories, but the Church is still a dangerous place for a gay priest.
Paperback: 978-1-78279-002-0 ebook: 978-1-78099-999-9

Do You Need God?
Exploring Different Paths to Spirituality Even For Atheists
Rory J.Q. Barnes
An unbiased guide to the building blocks of spiritual belief.
Paperback: 978-1-78279-380-9 ebook: 978-1-78279-379-3

Readers of ebooks can buy or view any of these bestsellers by clicking on the live link in the title. Most titles are published in paperback and as an ebook. Paperbacks are available in traditional bookshops. Both print and ebook formats are available online.

Find more titles and sign up to our readers' newsletter at
www.collectiveinkbooks.com/christianity
Follow us on Facebook at
https://www.facebook.com/ChristianAlternative

Also in This Series

Quaker Quicks - Practical Mystics
Quaker Faith in Action
Jennifer Kavanagh
ISBN: 978-1-78904-279-5

Quaker Quicks - Hearing the Light
The core of Quaker theology
Rhiannon Grant
ISBN: 978-1-78904-504-8

Quaker Quicks - In STEP with Quaker Testimony
Simplicity, Truth, Equality and Peace - inspired by
Margaret Fell's writings
Joanna Godfrey Wood
ISBN: 978-1-78904-577-2

Quaker Quicks - Telling the Truth About God
Quaker approaches to theology
Rhiannon Grant
ISBN: 978-1-78904-081-4

Quaker Quicks - Money and Soul
Quaker Faith and Practice and the Economy
Pamela Haines
ISBN: 978-1-78904-089-0

Quaker Quicks - Hope and Witness in Dangerous Times
Lessons from the Quakers On Blending Faith, Daily Life, and Activism
J. Brent Bill
ISBN: 978-1-78904-619-9

Quaker Quicks - In Search of Stillness
Using a simple meditation to find inner peace
Joanna Godfrey Wood
ISBN: 978-1-78904-707-3